# Nootka &
# Kyuquot
# Sounds

## Heather Harbord

*To Caroline Stoddart*
*a wonderful paddling companion*

Rocky
Mountain Books
Calgary–Victoria–Vancouver

*Front cover: Fog rolls in to Kyuquot.*
*Back cover: Photo of Heather Harbord by Lorna McCahon.*
*All pictures by the author unless otherwise credited.*

We acknowledge the financial support of the Government of Canada through the Book Publishing Industry Development Program (BPIDP) and the support of the Alberta Foundation for the Arts for our publishing program.

Copyright © 2004 Heather Harbord

Printed in Canada

Published by
Rocky Mountain Books
#106, 17665-66A Avenue
RMB  Surrey, BC  V3S 2A7

**National Library of Canada Cataloguing in Publication**

Harbord, Heather, 1939-
    Sea kayak Nootka & Kyuquot Sounds / Heather Harbord.

Includes index.
ISBN 1-894765-52-4

    1. Sea kayaking--British Columbia--Nootka Sound--Guidebooks.
2. Nootka Sound Region (B.C.)--Guidebooks. I. Title.

GV776.15.B7H37 2004    797.1'224'097112    C2004-900732-7

# Contents

Introduction – 5
Acknowledgements – 8
Area Map – 10
Trip Rating – 12
Weather, Climate and Sea Conditions – 14
Natural History – 14
Trip Planning – 19
Land Ownership – 30
Paddling Etiquette – 32

**1. Nookta Sound – 34**
    1. Gold River to Matchlee Bay – 39
    2. Gold River to Mooyah Bay – 41
    3. Nesook Bay to Cougar Creek – 42
    4. Cougar Creek to Hisnit Inlet – 43
    5. Moutcha Bay to Cougar Creek – 45
    6. Cougar Creek to Friendly Cove – 46
    7. Tuta Marina to Friendly Cove – 50
    8. Cougar Creek to Friendly Cove via Hoiss – 53
    9. Friendly Cove to Tahsis – 57

**2. Esperanza Inlet – 59**
    10. Tahsis to Esperanza – 65
    11. Zeballos to Ehatisaht – 67
    12. Ehatisaht to Catala Island on North side of Esperanza Inlet – 69
    13. Little Espinosa and Espinosa Inlet to Esperanza Inlet – 71
    14. Esperanza to Steamer Point to Rosa Island – 74

**3. Nuchatlitz and beyond – 77**
    15. Rosa Island to Grassy Knoll – 81
    16. Rosa Island to Nuchatlitz lagoons – 84
    17. Grassy Knoll to Rosa Island via Port Langford portage – 85
    18. Grassy Knoll to Benson Point – 87
    19. Benson Point to the end of Inner Basin – 88
    20. Nuchatlitz to Tongue Point – 90
    21. Tongue Point to Third Beach via the lagoon – 93
    22. Rosa Island to Friendly Cove on the outside – 94
    23. Nuchatlitz to Catala Island Spit – 97

### 4. Catala Island – 98

24. Circumnavigation of Catala Island – 101
25. Catala Island to Queen Cove – 102
26. Queen Cove to the head of Port Eliza – 104
27. Catala Island to Yellow Bluff – 105
28. Yellow Bluff to Rugged Point – 106

### 5. Kyuquot Sound – 109

29. Fair Harbour to Rugged Point – 116
30. Fair Harbour to Kyuquot – 119
31. Fair Harbour to the Artlish and Tahsish Rivers – 121
32. Fair Harbour to the head of Kashutl Inlet – 125
33. Easy Inlet to Chamiss Bay and Kyuquot – 127
34. Rugged Point Beaches – as a hike – 129
35. Rugged Point to Grassy Island – 130
36. Rugged Point to fresh water on Union Island – 132
37. Rugged Point to Kyuquot – 133
38. Rugged Point to the Thornton Islands – 135
39. Thornton Islands to Spring Island – 140
40. Kyuquot to Spring Island – 143
41. Circumnavigation of Spring Island and the Mission Group – 144
42. Kyuquot to Lookout Island – 146

### 6. Bunsby Islands and South Brooks Peninsula – 147

43. Kyuquot to the Bunsby Islands – 150
44. Malksope Inlet – 152
45. Bunsby Islands to the Acous Peninsula – 154
46. Ououkinsh Inlet – 155
47. Battle Bay to Jackobson Point – 157
48. Jackobson Point to Johnson Lagoon and Nasparti Inlet – 158
49. Brooks Peninsula – Jackobson Point to Solander Island – 160

Useful Contacts – 163
Metric Conversions – 164
Treatment of Hypothermia – 165
Historical Chronology – 168
Further Reading – 169
Camping Checklist – 170
Footnotes – 172
Index – 173
In Case of Emergency – 176

# Introduction

Nootka and Kyuquot (pronounced ky-YOO-cut) Sounds are the next step for sea kayakers who have enjoyed the Gulf Islands, the Sunshine Coast, Desolation Sound and the Broken Islands. Its wetter weather and more rugged coastline offer greater challenges as well as the rewards of pristine sandy beaches, remote islands, sea caves, rare sea otters, and historic sites. Although not quite the wilderness it was in the days of the explorers and fur traders, for those with the necessary skills, it comes close to the age old Canadian dream of wilderness and freedom.

~

*On a typical day of sea kayaking in the Nootka and Kyuquot Sound areas, I wake up to the sound of birds and listen to the weather forecast as I dress and apply sun screen before leaving my tent. There's no wind as I cook breakfast and sit, coffee in hand, watching the sea otters dive for urchins or listen to the black oystercatchers screaming as they fly from rock to rock.*

*I pack lunch into my kayak and paddle out onto the smooth water enjoying the way the boat cleaves through it so effortlessly. The reflections of the clouds make me think I'm flying. Peering into the clear depths, I watch crabs and small fish dart in and out of the kelp. Mesmerized, I enjoy the peace.*

*When the wind gets up, I land on an island and explore it before finding a sheltered nook in which to eat and read. If it's a historic site, I think about the people who came before me—the*

*First Nations warriors, the eighteenth century explorers and traders. At low tide, I check out the myriad of life in the tide pools and look for green glass floats. After the tide has crept in over the warm shingle, I swim. As the wind begins to die, I paddle back to camp, cook supper and enjoy the sunset.*

*If I wake during the night, I check out the stars and the northern lights. If phosphorescence illuminates the shoreline, I get up and swim or paddle to enjoy the green halo surrounding every movement in the water.*

~

On the frequent occasions when the Rain God has forgotten to turn off the shower, the place is still enjoyable if you're dressed for the weather and your camp is sheltered with well set-up tarps. This is much wilder terrain than the sheltered Broken Islands or Gulf of Georgia. There are fewer landing spots and long stretches of coast exposed to the world's largest ocean. Off-season paddling is not recommended.

Friendly Cove in Nootka Sound played a major role in early British Columbia history. In 1778, Captain James Cook on his third round the world voyage visited it and became the first European to step ashore in the Pacific Northwest. Other explorers who came included Malaspina, Vancouver, Quadra and many of the people whose names occur all over the B.C. coast. Traders followed hunting the sea otter to extinction by 1800. By the end of the nineteenth century, the proud First Nation's whalers, whose graceful ten metre dugout canoes had plied the inlets for four thousand years, were decimated by smallpox and bureaucracy. Twentieth century loggers denuded many of the inlets of trees but a lush second growth masks this. Descendants of the original First Nations people still travel the inlets, but in modern craft.

The natural history of the area is also very special. Places like the Brooks Peninsula and some of the outer islands escaped the last ice age and consequently have a unique flora. Thirty years ago Alaskan sea otters were re-introduced to the Bunsby Islands and have now spread down the

---

**A Montrealer's Experience**

I met Celine Picard in Campbell River where she was waiting for West Coast Expeditions to pick her up. "I've never done anything like this before in my life," she said. "A friend of mine has been five times and got a group of us together. It sounds like a lot of fun." A week later, I ran into her on Spring Island hurrying to supper with a bottle of wine in her hand. "This isn't camping, it's luxury," she said. "Two of us share a giant tent with 15 cm-thick mattresses. I've been paddling a double kayak but I"m going to try a single tomorrow. Yesterday, the wind came up and we got stuck on an island but the guides just called the company's boat to come and rescue us. It's great to be able to rely on them to keep us safe because we know nothing about the sea." West Coast Expeditions is run by a marine biologist in conjunction with elders of the Kyuquot people. Few outfitters have their breadth of experience.

---

coast to Bajo Point on Nootka Island. Wolves, cougar and black bear (but no grizzlies) roam at will. If you're lucky, you'll meet them or see their footprints. Just after dawn, you may see a large brownish dog on the beach. Keep very quiet, it's a wolf. If it's not there, see if it has left footprints in any sandy areas or a series of hollows in small shingle.

Nootka and Kyuquot Sounds have long been popular with U.S. and overseas paddlers. Most are kindred spirits who are good for an evening chat or advice on current conditions. In addition, you'll meet the people who live out here all year round. Some have work at logging camps, fish farms, and sport fishing lodges but many don't. In the Nootka Sound area, there are also the lighthouse keepers at Friendly Cove and the Williams family on the reserve there. Tahsis and Zeballos are small communities which you'll mainly use as launches. Kyuquot is the only community with no road access. Call in for at least an ice cream and perhaps a look at native crafts.

Getting there is half the fun especially if you take the *MV Uchuck III*, a 41 metre coastal ship, which brings freight and passengers to all the little isolated communities and fish farms. Watch the crew unload and load all kinds of pipes, lumber, trucks, appliances and groceries. Enjoy fresh muffins and home made soup from the galley off the main saloon. Visit the wheelhouse (but don't get in the way.) Ask the captain about the current and expected weather patterns. Both Captain Fred Mather and his son, Sean, as well as the crew have been plying these waters for many years and have good advice for those who listen. For most of the passengers on the *Uchuck*, this voyage is the highlight of their trip. The kayak launching and pickups are part of their entertainment. Some passengers who have stayed overnight on the Kyuquot or Zeballos runs come back as kayakers when they see what fun it is.

Sea kayaking has become a popular sport drawing ever increasing numbers of paddlers out of the cities and into the wilderness. Kayaking the west coast is much more complicated than taking a walk in a park or even a paddle in the sheltered Gulf Islands. More training and knowledge are required. Once achieved, a whole new world opens up. The cities are replaced by rock and forest with occasional swaths of glorious beaches. Tides and weather rule this environment where birds and animals are more numerous than people. Stores and medical help are far away. Radios, satellite and cell phones do not work in many places. You need to solve your own problems. What you know is more important than who you know.

Long before venturing into these remote areas, study weather forecasting, navigation and seamanship. Practice surf landings and think carefully about how you can be selfsufficient. It''s easy for a group to get separated and help can be a long time arriving. If you lack the skills or the lead time, go with an outfitter employing qualified sea kayak guides who know the area. The rewards for the well-prepared paddler are great.

In this book, I have broken the area down into 49 trips. These are just suggestions for planning purposes. Once out there, wind and weather will dictate where you go depending on your skill level. You'll have a more comfortable trip if you read the weather and trip planning sections before you finalize too much. If necessary, add to the list of contacts at the end and take the book with you so that you have all this information to hand. Hopefully, you won't have to depend on the section on hypothermia while up an inlet with no VHF contact. The historical chronology will help keep events in perspective.

Camping up the inlets or on the outer coast far from telephones and work stress, you can relax and enjoy. Even stormbound wet days can be fun if you've brought enough books to read and perhaps a pack of cards. Or just sit on a log and think. It's amazing how objective you can be when totally removed from your usual environment.

# Acknowledgments

I greatly appreciate the help of many paddlers, friends, experts and advisors who assisted in many ways.

Thank you Caroline Stoddart who steadied my boat when I got in or out. Ate the worst meal I have ever cooked (although she did give the cat food to the dogs!) Rescued me from falling off a cliff at Rugged Point. Cooked and cooked and baked up a storm so that I could write up my notes. Thought we'd lost it by coming out to the Thornton Islands but quickly fell in love with them. Often helped me haul my gear up and down the beach.

Others who helped were:
Clyde Burton for his encyclopedic knowledge of birds. Tony and Jacquie Clayton who shared their paddling experiences especially on the outside of Nootka Island.

Ann Cooper who took the pictures and supplied first hand information about tackling the Brooks Peninsula as well as sharing her knowledge of hypothermia treatment.

Rick Davies, a proud "chicken," who advised on the hypothermia appendix and suggests setting up your trip so that help is right there. The De Vault families for their insights into the Nuchatlitz area and the Nootka Trail.

Blake Fougere who checked over the section on forest tenures. Ann Gumpoldsberger for information on Flynn Cove.

Martin and Esther Kafer who took some of the pictures and shared the fun. Phyllis Ogis who labelled all my slides.

Steve Schleicher who paddled to Grassy Island with my camera and took pictures. The Treen family who advised on the hypothermia appendix.

The *MV Uchuck* captain and crew who are a mine of local lore especially about weather conditions. Margaret Waddington who knows more about Northwest history than I ever will

Peter Waddington who took many of the pictures and has co-led many trips to this area. Jerry West of the Gold River Record, Sgt. Scott Patrick of the Canadian Rangers and the *Uchuck* crew who filled me in on the tragic story of the two men who drowned in Nuchatlitz Inlet in May 2003.

Rupert Wong for advice on Nasparti, Ououkinsh and Malkscope Inlets, and especially Tony Daffern for putting it all together.

## Disclaimer

There are inherent risks in sea kayaking. While the author has done her best to provide accurate information and to point out potential hazards, conditions may change owing to weather and other factors. It is up to the users of this guide to learn the necessary skills for safe paddling and to exercise caution in potentially hazardous areas. Please read the introduction to this book and, in particular study the Trip Rating guidelines on pages 8 and 9.

Paddlers using this book do so entirely at their own risk and the author and publishers disclaim any liability for injury or other damage that may be sustained by anyone using the access and/or paddling routes described.

*Beach at Rugged Point.*

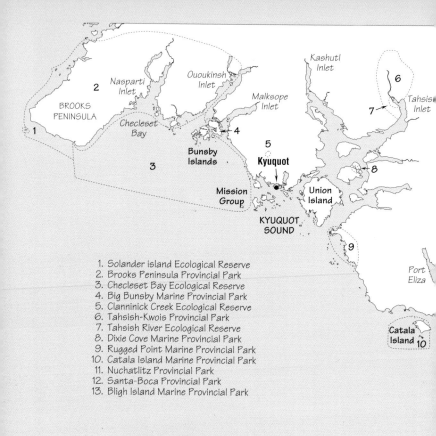

1. Solander island Ecological Reserve
2. Brooks Peninsula Provincial Park
3. Checleset Bay Ecological Reserve
4. Big Bunsby Marine Provincial Park
5. Clanninick Creek Ecological Reserve
6. Tahsish-Kwois Provincial Park
7. Tahsish River Ecological Reserve
8. Dixie Cove Marine Provincial Park
9. Rugged Point Marine Provincial Park
10. Catala Island Marine Provincial Park
11. Nuchatlitz Provincial Park
12. Santa-Boca Provincial Park
13. Bligh Island Marine Provincial Park

# Nookta Sound
# &
# Kyuquot Sound

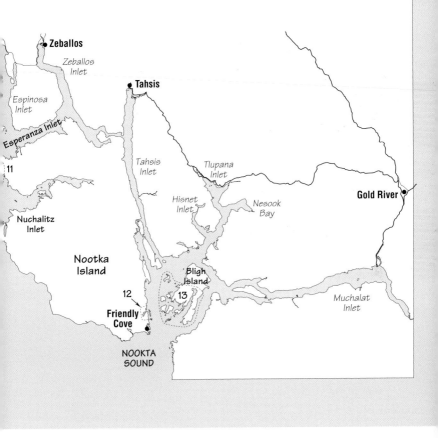

Vancouver Island

Zeballos

Zeballos Inlet

Tahsis

Espinosa Inlet

Esperanza Inlet

11

Nuchalitz Inlet

Tahsis Inlet

Tlupana Inlet

Hisnet Inlet

Nesook Bay

Gold River

Nootka Island

12

Bligh Island

13

Friendly Cove

Muchalat Inlet

NOOKTA SOUND

N

# Trip Rating

Routes described in this guide have been rated according to the paddling skills required, normal sea and shoreline conditions and the level of risk normally associated with such conditions. The rating given to a trip is an indication of what to expect in good, summer conditions. It is an assessment of risk, taking into account paddling skill level and difficulties likely to be encountered.

**Difficulty** is a measure of sea conditions: wind, waves, currents, tide rips and length of open–water crossings, and shoreline conditions: surf and infrequent and/or difficult landings.

**Risk** is the possibility of inconvenience, discomfort, injury or even loss of life. For the paddler, the level of risk is not constant. Along the same route and with the same paddling conditions, different paddlers will encounter different levels of risk. For a beginner, risky conditions may include small wavelets that arise before white–capped waves appear. For a more skilled paddler the same waves may hardly be noticeable. Risk can be reduced by good paddling skills, knowledge and judgement. Risk is increased in worsening conditions, remote locations and with poor decision–making.

There is a complex relationship between paddling skills, difficulty and risk. The individual paddler's skill level, the nature of the route, changing weather, and the presence of a competent leader are essential factors in determining the difficulty and risk of a sea kayak journey.

Sound decision–making is critical to the enjoyment and safety of sea kayaking touring and an experienced leader will often reduce difficulty and risk to acceptable levels. In the company of a skilled leader, a beginner can paddle safely along a coast rated intermediate. With good leadership a large portion of the Gulf Islands coastline is accessible to beginner–level paddlers and a coastline rated as "advanced" is by no means the sole domain of the advanced paddler.

The rating descriptions below cover many, but not all of the factors required to assess difficulty and risk. There may be other factors to be considered such as river outflows, reflected waves, the profile of a surf beach and the limitations of gear and cold water.

The skill–levels referred to below correspond to the conditions i.e. intermediate paddlers have the attributes necessary to safely travel in intermediate conditions.

**Novice conditions – minimal risk**
- Sheltered locations with stable conditions.
- Wind calm (less than 8 knots); sea state calm to rippled.
- Travel is along shore with abundant easy landing sites.
- Frequent opportunities for communication and road access; assistance is nearby.

Trip Rating courtesy Doug Alderson.

A group of novice paddlers can travel safely on day trips along the shore. Poor decisions or misinterpreting changing weather or sea conditions is unlikely to cause harm or significant inconvenience.

## Beginner conditions – low risk
- Mostly sheltered locations with stable conditions.
- Light winds (0–11 knots) current (0–0.5 knots) Sea state calm to light chop.
- Abundant easy landing sites and short open crossings less than 1.5 nmi.
- Frequent opportunities for communication and access; assistance may be up to an hour away.

A group of beginners can travel safely on day trips. Intermediate paddlers familiar with the area could lead beginners on an overnight trip. Poor decisions or misinterpreting changing weather or sea conditions is likely to cause inconvenience but unlikely to cause harm.

## Intermediate conditions – moderate risk
- A complex open water environment with the potential for moderate change in conditions.
- Moderate winds (12–19 knots); sea state moderate with wind waves near 0.5 meters; surf less than 1 meter; current less than 3 knots.
- Intermittent landing opportunities with some difficult landing sites; open water crossings less than 5 nmi (nautical miles).
- Communication may be interrupted; assistance may be more than one hour away.

A group of intermediate paddlers can travel safely on day trips. Advanced paddlers familiar with the area could lead intermediate paddlers on an extended overnight trip. Poor decisions or misinterpreting changing weather or sea conditions is likely to cause great inconvenience, the need for external rescue and possibly personal harm.

## Advanced conditions – considerable risk
- Complex open water environment with frequently changing conditions.
- Continuous exposure to wind, swell or current.
- Strong winds (near 20 knots); sea state rough with wind waves near 1 metre; surf greater than 1 metre or tide rips greater than 3 knots are routine.
- Infrequent landing opportunities with some difficult landing sites; open water crossings greater than 5 nmi
- Remote locations where communications can be difficult or unavailable; assistance may be a day or more away.

A mix of intermediate and advanced paddlers can travel safely on day trips. On extended overnight trips all paddlers should have advanced skills. Poor decisions or misinterpreting changing weather or sea conditions is likely to cause personal harm, without the availability of prompt external rescue.

# Weather, Climate and Sea Conditions

## Weather

The best months for sea kayakers are July and August. June and September are shoulder months. October through May are off season and conditions can be perilous.

On the West Coast, weather and tides rule your life. Carry a weather radio and listen to the marine forecast religiously before setting out every morning and several times during the day. Use a weather radio for the forecasts instead of depleting the batteries of your VHF radio which need a lot of battery power to transmit. Except in the inlets, Tofino Coast Guard Radio weather reports come in loud and clear boosted by the repeater station at Eliza Dome. This same station makes it easy to contact the Coast Guard on Channel 16 in an emergency. Weather forecast regions for this area are Vancouver Island South and Vancouver Island North. The dividing line between the two is Tatchu Point. If you're near it, heed both forecasts.

Wind is the most important weather phenomenon for kayakers. Around the outer points, it will be stronger than on straight shorelines. In warm weather, the land heats up more than the sea causing air to be sucked inland during the daytime and out to sea at night. These inflow–outflow winds can kick up big waves even at the head of the inlets. If caught by them, land and wait till dawn or dusk. Sometimes they will die down during a tide change. In the inlets off Nootka Sound, wind funnels round points never letting up and bullying you just when you think you have some shelter. Often, it is too windy to paddle between 10 am and 6 pm. Even strong paddlers make no headway in seventeen knots of wind or greater. Wind and waves are stronger than you, don't fight them. Enjoy your time ashore. Relax in the sunshine letting the pebbles run through your fingers as you watch sea otters play.

Sea fog is a problem especially in August. The low line of cloud hovering offshore is often a fog bank just waiting to blanket the shore. It arrives fast and can be so thick that visibility drops to 10 metres. Worse, it can bring a strong south wind with it with little or no warning. Keep warm clothes to hand in your boat in case you have to put them on in a hurry to ward off hypothermia (see page 165).

In places like Nuchatlitz Inlet, inflow winds combined with an ebb tide create high waves and chaotic seas which are hard to paddle in. The same thing happens at the mouth of Kyuquot Sound and any place where a large inlet empties into the ocean.

During the winter before your trip, study Owen Lange's *Living with Weather along the British Columbia Coast*[1]. Pay particular attention to the section on West Vancouver Island. Buy a weather radio and listen to your local forecasts till you become familiar with the meteorological terms used. Look out the window and watch the sky as a front passes through. Reading the first part of Lange's book explains some of the variables which makes it almost impossible to produce up-to-the-minute forecasts. A

*Brooks Peninsula in fog.*

combination of listening and looking at the sky will show you that often the forecasts should be respected. The weather sometimes comes in faster or slower than predicted. Weather knowledge is more important than anything else on the west coast.

### Average Temperature and Precipitation

Summer months have daytime temperatures in the low 20 degrees Celsius but can reach up into the 30s. Winters are wetter with temperatures around 12 °C. Between 1978 and 2001, Nootka light station reported only 12 years in which the temperature dipped below -2 °C. They reported an average of 15 cm of snow per year.

Average annual total precipitation is approx 4,000 mm. July and August have the least rain.

Average sea temperature is 6-8 °C in January and 14-16 °C in July. Predicted survival time in water of 10 °C is 2½ to 3 hours. You'll only be able to swim a tenth of the distance you can cover in a warm swimming pool. Wet suits and dry suits increase survival time.

### Sea Conditions

The outer coasts are subject to Pacific Ocean swells and the very occasional tsunami, which is another reason for regularly listening to weather forecasts. Swells can build up many miles out to sea and persist long after the storm which produced them has moved on. Even a low surf can make landing difficult. If you capsize when trying to land with a loaded boat, quickly move to one end of the hull so that the boat doesn't beat you to a pulp as the waves drive it up the beach and suck it out again.

In July and August, the lowest tides will be around 0 or chart datum and the highest up to 11.8 feet. Of the four tides each day, there is a high high tide and a low high tide. Similarly with the lows, one is a high low tide and the other a low low tide. When choosing campsites, remember that wind and swell on top of a high tide can push the water farther up the beach. Learn to look for the lines of seaweed marking the last high high tide. Should the water suddenly recede below the lowest tide you expect, listen to the radio for a tsunami warning and get to high ground. Unlike the Gulf Islands or Johnstone Strait, currents are not a problem in this area.

To avoid confusing backwash from cliffs, paddle farther out. When going through a group of rocky skerries watch the sideways sucking action of the waves ahead of you. If you get too close to a skerry, you may be washed up on a ledge and unable to get off before your boat is pounded to pieces. Study the rock symbols given in Chart No. 1. A star symbol indicates a rock which will be above the water at high tide. This is easy but check the chart for plus signs. Those with four dots mark the location of rocks that appear above water at low tide. An unadorned plus sign indicates a rock just below the surface at low tide. At various tide levels, a wave can easily slam your boat down on one of these cracking or holing it. This is when you need duct tape and a fibreglass repair kit that will work under water. Look ahead and avoid these potential hazards whenever possible.

*Cutting it fine. Tide almost reached the tent.*

# Natural History

Limestone topography in a number of places results in caves, mainly inland near Gold River and Tahsis, but also in cliffs along the inlets. Fossiliferous outcroppings occur on beaches around Rugged Point and up to Kyuquot. Check the rocks for several kinds of bivalve shells as well as ammonites and belemnites in these areas.

The Brooks Peninsula and Grassy Island near Rugged Point escaped glaciation. Flora on the spine of the Brooks Peninsula is similar to flora on central ridges of South Moresby Island in the Queen Charlottes. Taylor's saxifrage (*Saxifraga taylori*) and Newcombe's Butterweed (*Senecio newcombei*), which occur in both places, are all that remain of a more widespread coastal flora decimated by the glaciers.

Remnants of the glorious sandy beaches of California, Oregon and Washington emerge for short distances on the outside of Nootka Island, between Kapoose Creek and Rugged Point and in a few places along the south coast of the Brooks Peninsula. Approximately 95 percent of the coast, especially in the interior inlets, is edged either with rocky boulders or cliffs. Landings can be difficult to impossible.

Birds like pigeon guillemots, and black oystercatchers rejoice in the rocky terrain. Bald eagles abound. Except around human settlements, gulls are relatively scarce. Amongst the ubiquitous Glaucous-winged hybrids, look for California and Heerman's gulls. Marbled murrelets, rhinocerous auklets, and puffins are seen in some locations.

Care should be taken not to get so close that the birds fly off their nests leaving them open to predators. Keep back about 500 metres. Nesting season is April to August, sometimes longer. Ocean birds take a long time to incubate their eggs and raise their young. Some species are close to extinction. Offshore islands and open ocean crossings sometimes bring opportunities to see pelagic birds such as murres, shearwaters and petrels.

On shore, Swainson's and Hermit thrushes sing, ravens croak and northwestern crows will attack any

---

### Endangered Colonial Nesters

Red-listed. Indigenous species or subspecies that have been legally designated or are being considered for legal designation as extirpate, endangered or threatened status in B.C.

Brandt's cormorant
Common murre
Double-crested cormornant
Horned puffin
Pelagic cormorant
Thick-billed murre

Blue-listed. Indigenous species or subspecies considered to be Vulnerable in B.C. They are at risk, but not extirpated, endangered, or threatened.

Ancient murrelet
Cassin's auklet
Tufted puffin

*Black bear at Benson Beach. Photo: Peter Waddington.*

food or wineskin left out overnight. Fox sparrows hop from log to log and cheekily scratch around your kitchen area if you sit quietly.

Once dusk descends, hoards of mice come out from under beach logs and boulders. Because of the danger of the incurable hantavirus, make sure that there is no food or dirty pots for them to contaminate. The isolated beaches are home to black bear, wolves and cougar. Unless you get up very early, you may only see their tracks. Sea otter are coming back from extinction on the outer coasts and competing with the native people for clams and other shellfish. Grey whales migrate up and down the coast and you may also see orca, minke whales, harbour porpoise, seals, sea lions and, occasionally, the oversized noses of elephant seals.

In summer, the lowest tides are in the daytime revealing a host of colourful creatures stranger than science fiction: scarlet blood stars, huge many-armed purple and orange sunflower stars, orange cup corals, purple sponges, scarlet and brown anemones, orange and brown sea cucumbers, Monterey sea squirts, decorator crabs, pelagic and goose necked barnacles and a host of others.

Above the high tide line, white oxeye daisies, orange Indian paintbrush, pink nodding onion, blue-eyed grass, giant sedges and many others proliferate.

# Trip Planning

Select the group to go. Limit the size to 4-6 people maximum. Put latecomers on a wait list. They could travel as a second group a week later. Choose experienced paddlers who:

- habitually listen to the marine forecast and know how to interpret it
- can paddle strongly against at least a 20 knot wind
- know and have practiced rescues
- can read charts and use a compass
- know how to ferry glide across a current
- know the marine rules of right of way
- if paddling in the lead, will check back frequently for others
- can make surf landings (or be restricted in where you can go.)

If paddling alone, you should be both experienced and skilled. Plan for a wider margin of safety. How many of the maneuvers in the section on hypothermia could you carry out on your own? Which self rescue techniques have you practiced well enough to be able to perform them in choppy seas? Who will call the Coast Guard if you don't come back and when?

July and August are the best months to visit the west coast. Temperatures which are equable all year can be warm to hot in these months. Precipitation is less likely but all-wet weeks are still a possibility. Storms are fewer.

Plan to be at the take-out a day early. This is the time to do short local trips that you can easily get back from if the wind comes up.

*Sunset in the skerries.*

*Big surf running at Friendly Cove.*

Depending on where you are going, consider taking a water taxi one or both ways to maximize time in choice areas. Make sure the group has enough cash between them to pay the water taxi. Gas is expensive out here and these boats use a lot of it.

Are you going to set up a base camp and make daily forays from it or are you going to move every night? If so, plan to not move every third day. Lugging all that stuff up and down the beach gets tiring **and** this is a way of building in a safety day in case you are storm stayed. If this happens early in the trip, be prepared to adjust your plan. Perhaps you won't be able to get as far afield as you'd hoped this year. If you don't drown, you can come back.

Consider moving at dawn and dusk or when the tide changes. Often winds diminish at these times.

Before leaving home, assemble the charts on a large table and using parallel rules pencil in proposed routes along with magnetic compass courses in both directions. This saves fiddling in fog. Fold your charts so that they will not only fit into your waterproof case but will show a full day's paddle at a time—or at least minimize the number of times you have to undo and refold them. Make sure everyone has a chart and knows how to read it and how to use a compass. This is still important even if you are using a GPS.

GPS owners will want to enter the latitude and longitude coordinates of prospective destinations before leaving home. On the water, they can tell how far they have to paddle to each one and how fast they are going. These instruments are very useful in the kind of thick fog which often blankets the coast in summer. They can also be used to accurately retrace a course.

Establish who will bring water-proofed VHF radios and ask them to get their proficiency certificates. Who will bring weather radios?

Know how long your group likes to paddle in a day. Most vacationing groups prefer to paddle 6-8 nmi, sometimes 10-12. They want time to relax and enjoy the area as well as travel. Leave the 25 nautical mile days to the hotshots. If the wind pattern is such that paddling is impossible between 9 am and 5 pm, you may not be able to go far safely. Some years

it's like this. Plan for it. Anything else is gravy.

Tell the group members that no one should have a pressing appointment the day after they take-out. Accidents happen most frequently when someone has to be somewhere at a set time. Build in a day's safety factor.

Appoint someone not going on the trip to be a contact person for the Coast Guard. This person should have the names, addresses and descriptions of all members of the party and their boats plus some idea of their skills. If you're going on the *MV Uchuck*, they will require this before they let you launch. They will launch you anywhere but will only pick you up at designated points. Even with high powered binoculars, kayaks are very hard to spot at a distance.

*Chef's hors d'oeuvres with reconstituted dried Moroccan lamb stew and sea asparagus.*

*Captain Fred Mathers in the wheelhouse of MV Uchuck III.*

During crossings, plan to keep the group together so that they are visible to other traffic. The lead boat is responsible for keeping the group together—the slow ones wouldn't be straggling if they could keep up the pace set by the racers ahead. Lead boats should look back at the rest of the group frequently. If this tactic doesn't work, the leader should have the boats paddle side by side in designated spots (for example Bob, you'll paddle between Jane and Sue). Each boat stays within easy talking distance of the others. However, in heavy seas, don't get too close to each other. Perhaps you should have remained stormbound on the last island.

Make sure everyone going has had a Tetanus shot within the last ten years. Plan what first aid items each person will carry.

Ask for volunteers to bring a bird book, a flower book, a tide pool book, star charts etc.

Consider drying your own food to take with you. Start months before and dry meal leftovers. Don't forget vegetables. Home-dried food is much cheaper and reduces weight to be loaded and unloaded or hung in a tree.

In addition to mandatory safety gear, put together a kayak repair kit including duct tape, fibreglass or kevlar repair and rudder repair kits. A pair of vicegrips and some odd bits of neoprene with glue are useful.

Fishing licenses are required both for fishing with a rod and for collecting shellfish. Find out if there is a PSP ban. If fishing with a rod, carry a net or gaff and something to put the fish in once you've caught them.

## Shake-down Trip

Do a weekend shake-down trip with the group. Listen to the marine forecast, not the land TV forecast, and talk about it with the group.

Review rescue procedures and have everyone practice them. Discuss how to recognize and treat hypothermia, the greatest killer of kayakers. (See page 165) Practice the H.E.L.P. and HUDDLE positions.

Let everyone see how easy or difficult it is to pack their kayaks and set up camp. Does anyone have any particularly useful equipment which the others would like to acquire before the big trip?

Try a food hanging session to show how easy or difficult it is with your equipment. How would this work under different conditions—an absence of trees, pouring rain, high winds?

## Being Stormbound

Enjoy the opportunity to set up camp properly, bake bread, make cinnamon buns, build a beach sauna, tell stories, read books, go for walks, watch birds, examine intertidal life, wash clothes, practice Tai Chi, write poetry etc. Above all, relax. You can't go anywhere and no one starves on this coast with all the sea vegetables to stew and the shellfish to roast—or eat raw.

## Off-season Paddling

Not recommended except for the most skilled and then only with extreme caution. The weather pattern in winter is different. Storms come up in minutes and don't let up for days. Winter tides are higher, rendering beach campsites unusable.

Two paddlers who attempted the outside of Nootka Island in May 2003, died. They were described as "experienced kayakers who were familiar with the Nootka Sound area." Another paddler was marooned on the Thornton Islands for the whole month of May one year. A man whose job it is to secure fish farms from breaking apart during storms said, "This coast has the worst weather in the world in winter. You get 10 metre swells and higher which will pick you up and dash you against the rocks again and again. Even if you have a wet suit, you don't have a chance. It will break your bones and the barnacles will shred a survival suit. Then there's the problem of finding a place to land. It's all rock. You really have to plan."

## Packing

Pack before leaving home. Repackage to remove excess paper and waterproof each item. If you have to eat a hurried meal in pouring rain, you should only have to open the items you're going to eat. If necessary, snip cooking instructions off packages and re-pack in ziploc bags—or write cooking instructions in waterproof ink on each bag. It pays to have a good supply of freezer quality small ziploc bags on hand when you start. They can often be re-used and later double as garbage bags.

After all the individual bags —kitchen bag, cockpit bag, food bags etc. are packed—assemble everything which is going in one pile as if you were going to load your boat in camp. Take two large net bags (1 metre long if possible) or light-weight nylon bags which, when empty can be crushed up in a corner, and fill them with small

### Read the Labels Before Packing

Rugged Point was the scene of my worst cooking disaster. In the past, I have often held over dried food from one year to the next—no more. I cooked up some old noodles topped with what should have been a delicious cashew-ginger sauce. Unfortunately, both the noodles and the cashews had gone rancid. To save the day, I opened a can of tuna. It was the wrong colour. A close inspection of the label said "cat food." At home, people say I'm a good cook—but not that night!

items. This will reduce the number of trips up and down the beach you will have to make.

Take the kayak out to the back yard and assemble the gear beside it so that items going in the bow are piled

September storm at Friendly Cove.

*Kayaks ready to be loaded on the Uchuck at Gold River. Photo: Peter Waddington.*

beside the bow etc. Heavier stuff goes in the stern. Pack everything, stuffing the net bags in last. If possible avoid carrying anything on deck. Tarps, empty water containers and spare paddles are good candidates for this as it doesn't matter if a wave washes over them. Rope them on as you would at the launch. Put the first chart in the chart case along with tide tables and set up the deck load with flares

### Water

Carry enough water for three litres per day per person. This is for drinking or cooking—take salt water soap for washing yourself and cooking utensils in the sea. Filter it before use. Even in remote areas, sometimes *giardia* in streams can cause diarrhea. Fill up before launching or as soon as possible thereafter. Many islands have no water sources.

and pump within reach. Now sit in the boat. Have you left room for last minute fresh food purchases?

Unpack the boat straight into your vehicle. Add only an overnight bag with your paddling clothes and clean clothes for when you return. Load the kayak itself and secure.

If travelling on the *MV Uchuck*, arrive at the dock by 5 pm the previous day and ask the office for instructions. These will vary depending on their load and schedule which often they don't know until the last minute. You may be asked to load the kayak on the dock. The crew will stow it on board later after their supper. They like you to keep heavy items out until just before they launch you so that they can move the boat from the side decks to the launch pad easily.

If a lot of boats are going out at the same time, the procedure is different. They will be stacked empty in the hold. Your gear will be stowed on deck in piles, so the fewer containers the better—the net bags are a great asset. You'll be loading at top speed so the rehearsal in the back yard will really pay off as you will be able to stow everything without hesitating.

## Wet Weather Camping

**Tarps** Set the tarps up first. Slant them so that rain pours off the side least used. Pitch your tent, which should be almost completely covered by its own fly, under a tarp so that it is completely covered. Having extra line to tie to distant trees and logs pays off. Use driftwood or paddles to raise the ceiling. It also helps to have a structural engineer, a.k.a. tarpmeister, in the party who knows how to put up tarps that stay up and don't flap in a wind. Contribute the second tarp to a communal kitchen area. Take extra grommets for repair jobs.

**Rain Gear** All rain gear should be seam sealed. Check the seals before leaving home. Breathable rain gear is apt to leak in the kind of heavy continuous rain, perhaps for days on end, which occurs even in summer on the west coast. It's a rain forest. Don't worry if you sweat inside your rain gear. That's what polypropylene underwear which wicks the moisture away from your skin is for. In warm weather, that and watertight rain gear is all you need.

*Tarpmeister Peter Waddington in action.*

*Tied up for the night at Easy Inlet.*

**Ziploc Bags** For food especially, pack anything you don't want to get wet in ziploc bags of various sizes. One item per bag or one bag for the item in use. Keep the rest, of the powdered drink or whatever, safely dry in a larger bag.

**Drying Out** Not likely, though I've singed a few sets of underwear trying. Hanging towels etc. up under tarps isn't productive when the air is moist. They end up wetter. Take clothes which are warm when wet like fleece and wool. No cottons. At night, pack day clothes into a dry bag. If the tent leaks, they'll still be dry. Try to keep one set of clothes dry at all costs. Put rain gear on as soon as it starts to rain and before your clothes get sodden.

Then when the warm sun comes out, quickly unpack everything and spread it over the hot shingle and logs. Tents flown as kites dry out quickly.

## Human Waste

If you want to make money, invent a gadget small enough to stow in a kayak to evaporate human waste without polluting either the atmosphere or the environment. Hurry up!

The alternatives are explored in Kathleen Meyer's *How to Shit in the Woods*. Ten Speed Press, 1989. ISBN 0-89815-319-0. Some BC Parks pamphlets recommend using the tideline away from shellfish beds. With increasing numbers of campers, this is no longer a good solution. At the least, groups should dig a biffy well away from camp and water sources. Consider storing and burning used toilet paper and tampons in a fire below the high tide line—or substituting the toilet paper with non-poisonous leaves or smooth rocks. As of 2004, it is mandatory for commercial sea kayaking operations to use boom boxes.

## Hot Weather

Use the tarps to provide shade. Wear long-sleeved cotton shirts, long lightweight cotton pants, sunhats and neckerchiefs. Pack waterproof sunscreen of 30 or higher and put it on exposed skin before leaving the tent in the morning. Carry and drink lots of water when paddling. You're more likely to get rain than hot water, but you never know.

## Campsites

Choice is usually limited so start looking around 3 pm and take the first one. In summer, the tide will be lower in the morning. Watch that there isn't a drop-off preventing a low tide launch or be prepared to wait. Avoid camping within 90 m (300 ft) of a fresh water source. Not only to avoid pollution, but also to keep wildlife well away.

Use established sites whenever possible and avoid creating new ones. Be prepared to share the site with others, especially if they arrive late in the day or in bad weather. The west coast is no longer a wilderness experience but often an opportunity to meet some very nice people with similar interests. Recently, guides of commercial trips now have to be licensed by the provincial government to use certain areas but do not have exclusive use of them. If you are camped in their favourite place, they should not ask you to leave.

Unload or carry loaded? This depends on the sea conditions. With carrying straps, four people can carry a loaded boat up the beach but two people often risk injury doing this. Find three thin logs and use them

Four person carry.

*Tarp palaces at Nuchatliz. Photo: Martin Kafer.*

as rollers to push the boats up one by one. Even solo paddlers can do this except on steep banks like that at Catala Island. Once the boats are unloaded, **always** tie them up. Are you sure where the high tide came to last night? Do the tide tables say it will come higher tonight? Is there any extra surge from an approaching storm or passing boat which could push it several feet higher?

Is there room to make a communal kitchen? Where can a hole be dug for grey water disposal?

Where is the biffy going to be?

Use stoves and fuel for cooking, especially in dry weather when sparks can easily set a whole beach of logs alight. Gather driftwood only for the garbage fire. Locate it downwind and

below tide. Never against a log. Pour water on it each night before going to bed. In the morning, collect up and crush any burned cans and pack them out. Wash plastic containers and pack them out instead of burning them. Should you carry an army hammock with mosquito netting and a tarp roof? Although hammocks are bad for people with back problems, they are useful if the only alternative is lumpy rocks. Sling an extra regular tarp over the top to keep all gear dry and form a shelter you can move about in.

Before leaving a campsite, always return poles used to erect tarps to their original places on the beach so that it looks untouched. Pack out all garbage and fill in the biffy.

# Land Ownership

In addition to private ownership, there are ecological reserves, parks, forest tenures and Indian Reserves.

## Indian Reserves

Six centuries and more ago when First Nation's canoes swept down from the north after the ice ages, they camped where they pleased which is why Indian Reserves often have two beaches for different kinds of weather. Before landing, ask permission at the Band Office of the First Nation concerned. They will give permission for some areas but not others.

## Ecological Reserves

These were created to preserve certain ecological treasures such as:

- representative samples of the province's ecosystems
- rare and endangered plant and animal species
- important genetic resources etc.

They are mainly used for scientific research and educational purposes. Our system of ecological reserves grew out of a ten year international biological program 1964-74 in which 58 nations participated, to identify representative terrestrial and aquatic ecosystems. In 1971, the BC legislature passed the Ecological Reserves Act giving permanently protected status to 29 reserves. Others have been added since. Camping is not allowed on ecological reserves except at designated sites.

## Provincial Parks

Most provincial parks in this area have been created in the last quarter century and are largely unorganized. BC Parks has a mandate to protect the natural environment including recreational values and representative and special natural ecosystems, species, features and phenomena. It has been doing this since 1911.

## Crown Land

Many different organizations can apply for short or long-term tenures of crown land. These are now being managed by Land and Water British Columbia Inc. (LWBC) a corporation of the government of British Columbia. Two tenures of interest to sea kayakers are commercial recreation tenures and forest tenures.

## Commercial Recreation Tenures[2]

Sea kayak guides operating on a fee-for-service basis must obtain a permit for non-exclusive use of specified areas. Some permits allow them to build "improvements" such as campsites. In these cases, LWBC grants them exclusive use of them.

Guides who hold both kinds of tenures are obligated to keep logs of their use for government inspection, pay fees and take out expensive liability insurance. Buried in their permit document is a statement saying that they "must not interfere with other campers on the Land"

My interpretation of this is that if non-fee groups are camped on the unimproved site of a commercial guide's tenure, they cannot ask you to leave.

*Skulls in cave on Second Island, Nuchatlitz.*

However, in the interests of peace and space permitting, it would be a good idea if you would graciously share the site. They have gone through a great deal of red tape to get it! It would also be helpful if the government would not give out tenures for small sites.

**Forest Tenures**

Under the Forestry Act, the B.C. government grants forest companies tree farm tenures to manage crown timber on a sustainable basis. Definitions of the terms and conditions of this and similar arrangements have been fought over for the better part of the last century. Basically, areas currently being logged have to be reforested within a time limit to a predetermined acceptable standard. The Ministry of Forests permits camping and picnicking in designated recreation sites.

**Private Land**

There's not a lot of private land in this area, but places like the Saavedra Islands, one of the islands at Nuchatlitz, and an area round Flynn Cove are privately owned. Ask permission before landing or camping.

# Paddling Etiquette

## Wildlife

**On the water** Carry waterproof binoculars so that you can see without getting too close. Frightened seals and sea lions can crush smaller animals when sliding into the water in a hurry to avoid you. The same is true of birds. If disturbed during nesting activities, gulls and other pelagic birds may give up altogether for the whole year. Back off before they start to move, especially if they are on nesting ledges.

**Ashore** If birds are pretending to be wounded they are trying to draw you away from nests on the ground. Watch where you place your feet and leave. The nests may be little more than shallow depressions in the shingle and very hard to see. Some birds nest in burrows so watch where you walk in grassy areas. Others have a pecking-order claim to cliff ledges.

If you see someone else watching or photographing birds or wildlife, do not make a noise or try to attract their attention. Never feed wildlife or leave scraps of food out for them. The bear or wolf you feed may attack the next visitor. When examining low tide creatures, put them back exactly where you found them, replacing protective seaweed or rocks gently.

## Dogs

Leave dogs at home. They chase shorebirds often destroying a year's nesting activities and they attract cougar and bear who regard them as tasty morsels. You're next—especially children!

*Black oystercatcher on nest.*

*Sea Otters. Photo: Martin Kafer.*

**First Nations Artifacts**

Many sites, including middens, are protected by the BC Heritage Conservation Act which heavily fines those who disturb or touch artefacts. For permission to visit, ask band offices not individuals.

**Local Residents**

Ask permission before landing on private property. Never take water from a pump without asking. It may be in short supply. If there's a store or restaurant, patronize it. Unemployment is 80% in some areas, notably Kyuquot, and they need all the business they can get.

**Other Paddlers**

Seek another beach if someone is there ahead of you, or land a distance away. Do not play loud radios or tapes or keep everyone awake by chatting round the fire when others within hearing distance want to sleep. In bad weather, assist others to land and launch and be gracious about sharing even a small campsite. It may be too dangerous for the newcomers, perhaps with less physical stamina than you, to continue.

# 1

# Nootka Sound

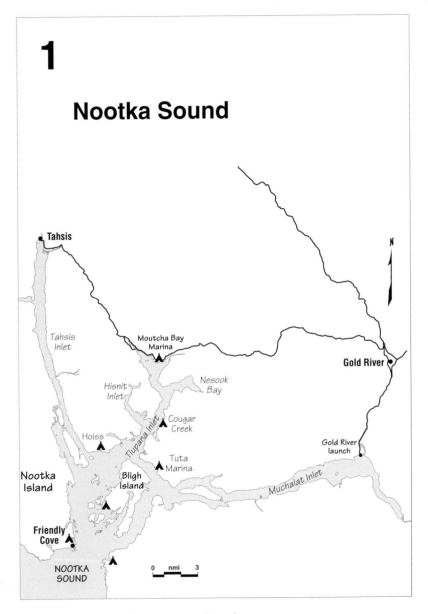

N

**Tahsis**

*Tahsis Inlet*

Moutcha Bay
Marina

*Nesook Bay*

**Gold River**

*Hisnit Inlet*

Cougar
Creek

Hoiss

*Tlupana Inlet*

Gold River
launch

Tuta
Marina

**Nootka
Island**

**Bligh
Island**

*Muchalat Inlet*

**Friendly
Cove**

NOOTKA
SOUND

0    nmi    3

Nootka Sound is the most historic area on the B.C. Coast. In 1778, Captain James Cook on his third round the world voyage, was the first European to step ashore. Battered by storms and desperate to replenish his wood and water, on the evening of March 29, he thankfully tucked his two ships in behind the point below Mount Adair and dropped anchor. In the morning, he sent Midshipman Bligh out in a longboat to find a more sheltered anchorage and later warped the ships over to Resolution Cove well away from the native village at Yuquot in case it proved to be unfriendly. He stayed a month and his accurate mapping forms the basis of today's charts.

A succession of explorers and fur traders followed. The Spanish established a settlement at Yuquot for a six year period during which they almost sparked a world war. Malaspina's 1791 scientific expedition mapped the inlets and José Mariano de Moziño, who accompanied Governor Bodega y Quadra the following year, documented natural history and First Nation's customs. Captain George Vancouver arrived in 1792 to restore British ownership, but wily American captains raised doubts about his claims, delaying resolution until four years later when the Spaniards packed up their settlement in favour of the British flag.

Bad trading practices led to a massacre of all but two of the crew aboard the Boston in 1802. Survivor, John Jewett, kept a diary of his enslavement which has been republished.

First Nation's people have lived here for over 4,000 years. Yuquot was the main village of a confederacy of the Nootka Sound people under Chief Maquinna. These people were one of the great whaling nations of the coast. They called the whales to their harpoons using the spirits in a shrine on an island in the lake behind their village.

There are two provincial parks in Nootka Sound. The southern half of Bligh Island along with the Villaverde Islands, Pantoja Islands, Verdia Island, Vernaci Island and Spouter Island are all part of Bligh Island Marine Provincial Park. Boca del Infierno, McKay Passage and Santa Gertrudis Cove are in Santa-Boca Provincial Park.

## Launches

### Gold River, Muchalat Inlet

Gold River is at the end of the only paved road access to Nootka Sound and therefore is popular with trailered

### The Great Walk

On the first Saturday in June the Tahsis road is closed for The Great Walk. Over a thousand people hike the 63 kilometres to Tahsis starting at 4 am. En route, they pass through twelve checkpoints and can drop out at any of them. Conuma campsite is the halfway point, lunch stop and a first-aid post with a doctor. When they reach Tahsis, firetrucks salute them as they pass under the symbolic burning boots and into the haven of the last checkpoint where mattresses on the floor provide overnight accommodation for those not bused back to Gold River.

boats. In fishing season, the launch is very busy. Kayakers should pack their boats elsewhere and carry them down to the water. The Mowachat people charge for launching and gated parking. Some free ungated parking is also available.

## *MV Uchuck III*

The *MV Uchuck III* is a 45 metre coastal freighter that has scheduled runs from Gold River at the head of Muchalat Inlet. In addition to freight of all kinds, it carries kayakers, canoeists and hikers. Kayaks and canoes may be taken aboard either loaded or unloaded (check with Nootka Sound Services on arrival) and launched loaded anywhere along the vessel's routes. Pick-up, however, must be at a designated port. Before launch, paddlers will be required to provide an approximate sail plan, and ETA for pick-up along with names and addresses of contact people in case of emergency. Only one such person is required for a group. This is a very valuable service which enables paddlers to avoid long, boring and sometimes hazardous paddles like those along Muchalat and Tahsis Inlets. Simple meals may be purchased from the cafeteria while on board. For further details of this and water taxi services from Gold River, see page 163.

## Nesook Bay, Tlupana Inlet

From the Gold River Visitor's Bureau, follow the signs for Tahsis. The pavement ends in about 2 kilometres. Cross the Gold River, and turn left. Cross another bridge and turn right up a hill. This is the Tahsis road. It is well maintained and well used. Twenty-six kilometres from Gold River a side

*Cove at northeast end of Bligh Island.*

## Moutcha Bay, Tlupana Inlet

From Gold River, follow the signs for Tahsis. Pavement ends in about 2 kilometres. Cross the Gold River, and turn left. Cross another bridge and turn right up a hill. This is the Tahsis road. It is well maintained and well used. Twenty-six kilometres from Gold River a side road branches off to the left down to Nesook Bay. Instead of taking this, continue on the main road to Tahsis for another 16 kilometres. The Conuma Valley is posted as an "archery only" hunting area. In season, the Campbell River Fish and Wildlife Association take over the campsite on the banks of the Conuma River. Though usually deserted, on occasion this campsite is heavily used as the mid-point of the Great Walk (see sidebar page 48).The Conuma Fish Hatchery is a kilometre farther on.

Moutcha Bay Resort (see page 163) is 42 kilometres from Gold River. Although it mainly caters to sportsfishers, it has lots of space for RVs and some places where tents may be pitched. The boat launch is up and over a hill past the small store and office. The advantage of launching here is that the campsite is a lot less busy than Cougar Creek and the Bay is usually calm. Kayakers are welcome. In fact, the owner rents kayaks and sponsors a kayak fishing derby.

road branches off to the left down to Nesook Bay (11 km), Cougar Creek (16 km) and Tuta Marina (19 km)[3] These are all potential launches.

Most people prefer to launch at Cougar Creek. Check how busy it is before choosing Nesook.

## Cougar Creek, Tlupana Inlet

From Nesook bay, continue five more kilometres. There is a sometimes crowded BC Forest campsite beside the launch.

## Tuta Marina, Hanna Channel

From Cougar Creek, continue three more kilometres. This part of the road is rough. Four wheel drive is an asset or drive very carefully and slowly. Tuta Marina is just north of the site of the Muchalaht village of Cheeshish. For details see page 163.

## Tahsis, Tahsis Inlet

From Gold River, follow the signs for Tahsis. Pavement ends in about 2 kilometres. Cross the Gold River, and turn left. Cross another bridge and turn right up a hill. This is the Tahsis road. It is well maintained and well used. At fifty-seven kilometers, watch for a

*Fallen totem pole, Friendly Cove.*

## Camping locations

**Cougar Creek** BC Forest Service site (40 units). Very busy in fishing season.

**Tuta Marina and Campgrounds** (29 sites) operates May-September, sometimes longer, see page 163.

**Friendly Cove** operated by the Mowachaht Band (18 wilderness tent sites, 6 cabins). For reservations contact Ahaminaquus Tourist Centre, see page 163.

**Hoiss** Unorganised. Approximately as large as Cougar Creek campsite.

**Tahsis** BC Forest Service campsite (8 units) on the Leiner River on the road to Tahsis. Otherwise, it is possible to camp behind the Bull of the Woods picnic site on the inlet just south of the boat launch.

Even for small groups of 2-3 tents, camp spots are hard to find. If you can't reach one of the above by about 3 pm, begin looking and take the first place you can find. Don't leave it until dusk.

**Bligh Island** Charlie's Beach at the southwest end of Bligh Island has room for 6-8 tents. Otherwise, camp spots are few, and park's staff warn that recently wolves have become more curious of campers and their belongings. Hang food and garbage. Never feed wild animal. Several years ago, campers on Vargas Island near Tofino were attacked by wolves after feeding them.

big Douglas fir tree on the right-hand side of the road. This is the President's Tree, a landmark beloved by Tahsis residents who know that they are nearing home when they pass it. The tree is named after Jack Christiansen, former president of Tahsis Company, who, when the road was being built, decreed that a sample big fir should be left.

Farther on, the green moss of the old-growth forest drenches the BC Forest campsite on the Leiner River and mutes the traffic noise from the road. Campers here are lulled to sleep by the river chuckling past their tents all night.

To reach the boat launch, follow the main road round the head of the inlet and through the town. Eventually, it comes down to a former hotel and some empty stores. The boat launch is just beyond.

# 1  Muchalat Inlet – Gold River to Matchlee Bay

**Difficulty**  Advanced conditions – considerable risk
**Distance**  5 nmi each way
**Duration**  4–5 hours
**Chart**  Nootka Sound No. 3675, depth in metres, scale 1:40,000
**Tides**  on Tofino
**Currents**  none

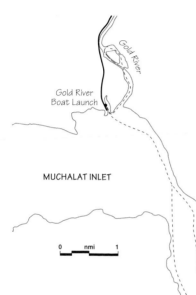

the inlet. Don't go unless the water is really calm. It's not worth the effort.

**Paddling Considerations**
- Inflow-outflow winds could be against you both ways and can be very strong. If they're raging, don't go.
- Steep cliffs edge much of the shoreline. When backwash from these is combined with strong winds, you need flexible hips and a vigilant eye to stay upright.
- Few landing places, so keep lunch and pee equipment within reach.
- No VHF reception.
- Other traffic near the launch includes sport fishers, commercial traffic like the *MV Uchuck*, and sea planes.

Fall is the most interesting time to do this trip as the salmon are returning to spawn and jump all around. Bald eagles feast on them in the boggy delta of the Burman River at the head of the inlet. The Muchalat people had villages in Matchlee Bay and at Ahaminaquus on the Gold River. This trip is mainly of interest to people who have been out on the *MV Uchuck* and want to see what's round the corner and the otherwise out-of-sight head of

## Muchalaht Wars

The Muchalaht people were blessed with two excellent salmon fishing rivers; the Gold and the Burman. Unfortunately, neighbouring tribes coveted them. The Muchalaht were attacked by the Nimpkish, the Mowachahts and the Ahousats and eventually retreated to two villages at Ahaminaquus and Matchlee on the Gold and Burman Rivers respectively. A proposed wedding between a Matchlee bride and the Mowachaht chief, cïwic, turned into a slaughter which decimated the village.

Later cïwic came again apparently in peace, but relatives warned the Muchalaht that he intended to kill their chiefs. After the feast a fight broke out during which the huge Muchalaht chief, anapinūł, picked cïwic up and slammed him down onto the rocks by the river. "I thought no one would dare to kill so great a chief as I,"cïwic gasped to which anapinūł replied: "You killed many of our people. This is the revenge of the Muchalaht." He continued to slam ciwic against the rocks till he died.

The Mowachahts retreated to Yuquot threatening revenge but were too fearful to exact it. Several years later a Muchalaht war party attacked and killed a Mowachaht berry picking party close to Yuquot. After this, the two tribes avoided each other. Around 1870, the Muchalaht chief invited the Mowachahts and the Ahousats to a big feast at Ahaminaquus and everyone agreed to stop the bloodshed.

### The Route

Before venturing out onto Muchalat Inlet, paddle about ten minutes up the Gold River. It's a pleasant side trip if there aren't too many sport fishers. Back at the river mouth, turn southeast along the shore of the inlet. At high tide there will be nowhere to land beneath the towering cliffs on either side. Once round the corner and out of sight of the remains of the pulp mill, there will probably be no other boats. Winds permitting, you may choose to cross the inlet to paddle up one side and return on the other. Landing on the shingle at the mouth of the Burman River is easy but finding a dry place to eat lunch may be problematical.

*Looking up Muchalat Inlet from the Gold River dock.*

# 2 Gold River to Mooyah Bay

**Difficulty** Advanced conditions – considerable risk
**Distance** 13.5 nmi one way.
**Duration** 5-6 hours
**Chart** Nootka Sound No. 3675, 1:40,000, depth in metres
**Tides** on Tofino
**Currents** none

Most people who consider doing this trip reconsider and take the *MV Uchuck* either to Mooyah Bay or some other place along the ship's route.

## Paddling Considerations
- Strong inflow-outflow winds
- Few landing places along the steep sided inlet. Keep lunch and pee equipment within reach.
- Steep cliffs in some areas
- Other traffic near the launch includes sport fishers, commercial traffic like the *MV Uchuck*, and sea planes – possibly also Luna, the too friendly orca.
- Crossing of Muchalat Inlet 0.5 nmi at the narrowest point between McCurdy Creek and Houston River.

## The route
Proceed down the north side of the inlet, past McCurdy Creek logging camp which is sheltered by a small islet. Either then or later, cross the inlet and sneak in behind the small islets off Houston River (a possible landing spot). Continue west along the shore to Ous Point. Paddle between it and the small islands at the east end of Gore Island. Pass Silverado Creek (another possible landing spot) and on to Mooyah Bay. This logging camp is not a good camp spot as the tide comes up into the sea grass. In an emergency there is almost always someone living at the camp with access to a radio. The *MV Uchuck* often docks here and can pick up kayaks. Watch for bears on the beach.

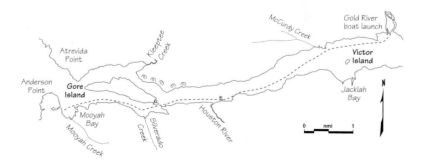

# 3 Nesook Bay to Cougar Creek

**Difficulty** Intermediate conditions – moderate risk
**Distance** 3.5 nmi one way.
**Duration** 1 hour
**Chart** Nootka Sound No. 3675, 1:40,000 depth, in metres
**Tides** on Tofino
**Currents** none

This is just a short hop in case Cougar Creek is jammed with sport fishers.

### Paddling Considerations
- Inflow-outflow winds
- Other traffic near the launch includes sports fishers.
- Crossings: none

### The route
The boat launch is at the west end of the log sort and from here the journey almost always starts in calm water. Once round Santa Saturnina Point, inflow-outflow winds may be encountered. The short paddle down the coast to Cougar Creek gives good views of the spectacular 300 metre cliffs guarding the entrance to Moutcha Bay.

*Nesook Boat Launch.*

# 4 Cougar Creek to Hisnit Inlet

**Difficulty** Intermediate conditions – moderate risk
**Distance**: 3.5 nmi one way.
**Duration** 1-2 hours
**Chart** Nootka Sound No. 3675, 1:40,000, depth in metres
**Tides** on Tofino
**Currents** none

The head of the inlet has a short hike to a lake. Nearby are the remains of a historic quarry.

## Paddling Considerations

- Inflow-outflow winds
- Watch for fast-moving sports fishing boats zipping in and out of the launch.
- Crossing: Cougar Creek to the northern shore of Tlupana Inlet 0.7 nmi.

## The route

From Cougar Creek, cross Tlupana Inlet and paddle southwest to the point opposite Argonaut Point. Then proceed up Hisnit Inlet. Valdes Bay is full of houseboats and there's almost nowhere to land unless you know someone. Close to the head of the inlet on the east side, grassy hummocks are all that remain of a quarry which supplied marble used in the construction of the Legislature in Victoria. The story following illustrates the hazards of camping there.

The 1.2 kilometre trail to Deserted Lake starts at the head of the inlet.

~

*At the head of the inlet, the tide had flooded the flat area we thought we could camp on. Reluctant to go farther, we squeezed five tents in between the shafts of the old limestone*

Cougar Creek launch.

quarry. It was one of those unlucky nights when the rain bucketed down. Being experienced campers, this didn't bother us. In fact, we had fun combining several large tarps into a shelter at one end of the fire. However, the wind started to gust and periodically doused the flames. The third time we retreated to warm sleeping bags. All night the wind blew like an express train. Rattle, rattle, bang. People groped their way out in the darkness, teetering on the quarry shaft edges while re-staking their tent pegs. Others listened snug in their warm bags.

Next morning I thought the little dog seemed uneasy but I said nothing. Three of us paddled over to Deserted River and walked up the trail to the lake which was full of logs. On the way back, we heard shouts. When we returned the others were waiting for us in their canoes about 6 metres offshore.

"A cougar came and snatched the dog," they explained. "Bob was standing within 3 m of the fire with the dog close by when he heard a sound and saw the cat with the dog in its mouth. He rushed after it, hollering and thrashing around. The cougar dropped the dog and took off. Your gear is all on shore." The dog had a couple of small teethmarks on its shoulder but was otherwise unharmed, although understandably quiet. Although cougars definitely live there, most people who visit Hisnit Inlet will never see one. It's a good idea to leave dogs at home and keep a close watch on small children.[4]

# 5 Moutcha Bay to Cougar Creek

**Difficulty** Intermediate conditions – moderate risk
**Distance** 4 nmi one way.
**Duration** 1.5 hours
**Chart** Nootka Sound No. 3675, 1:40,000, depth in metres
**Tides** on Tofino
**Currents** none

Moutcha Bay and adjacent Head Bay are relatively sheltered for paddling. Crossing Tlupana Inlet may not be. En route you pass below high sheer cliffs.

## Paddling Considerations

- Inflow-outflow winds
- Sports fisher traffic near launch
- Crossings
  – Perpendicular Bluff to the point just north of Princess Royal Point 0.5 nmi
  – Tlupana Inlet opposite Cougar Creek 0.7 nmi

## The route

It's usually possible to paddle straight across the bay, perhaps stopping to inspect the nets belonging to the Conuma Fish Hatchery at the mouth of the river or exploring the adjacent Head Bay where there used to be an iron mine and a log sort. The big attraction is the 300 metre cliffs of Perpendicular Bluff which drop sheer into the water.

After the sobering experience of paddling below this humbling sight, cross to Princess Royal Point. Continue down the coast below steep cliffs for 1.2 nmi and then cross the main channel of Tlupana Inlet to Cougar Creek. In season, watch for fast-moving sports fishers as you approach.

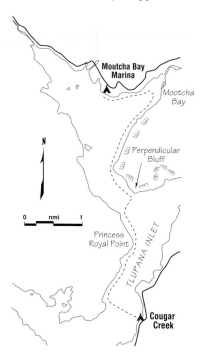

# 6 Cougar Creek to Friendly Cove via Bligh Island

**Difficulty** Intermediate conditions – moderate risk
**Distance** 11 nmi one way.
**Duration** 4 -5 hours
**Chart** Nootka Sound No. 3675, 1:40,000, depts in metres
**Tides** on Tofino
**Currents** none

Friendly Cove with its historic church, lighthouse and village remains is the attraction of this paddle.

## Paddling considerations

- Inflow-outflow winds tend not to be as strong as in the narrower inlets like Muchalat and Tahsis.
- Crossings
  – Descubierta Point to San Carlos Point on Bligh Island 0.7 nmi.
  – Clotchman Island in the Spanish Pilot Group to the Saavedra islands 1.1 nmi.
- Sport fishers launch at Gold River, Cougar Creek and Moutcha Bay and drive fast and furiously to their destinations. They congregate by Camel Rock at the mouth of Tlupana Inlet and off Friendly Cove which even they refer to as "the Zoo." Paddlers are easier to see if they cross open water in tight groups.
- Sea fog regularly steals in during the late afternoon. Plan to be ashore before this happens, but have compass courses marked on your charts in case the fog comes in quickly.
- Few landing places. If caught by the fog while still around Bligh Island, a small group could camp at Charlie's Beach on the inside of the southwest tip of Bligh between Verdia and Clotchman islands.

- Freighters come in to Nootka Sound and up Tahsis and Muchalat Inlets if the mills are operating.

## The route

Proceed down Tlupana Inlet and cross over to San Carlos Point on Bligh Island. In calm weather, explore the Villaverde Islands on the way and or the Spanish Pilot Group at the south end of Bligh. Take mosquito repellent if you go ashore. Watch for tiny sandy pocket beaches especially at low tide.

Take a moment to look back up Tlupana Inlet. The triangular peak is Conuma Peak. It was a welcome signpost for whaling canoes returning after several days hunting offshore.

From Narvaaz or Clotchman islands, cross over to the Saavedra Islands. This part of the journey is subject to swells from the open ocean but usually they are pretty muted. Once in the Saavedra Islands, it's a short paddle down to Friendly Cove where the Band charges a landing fee as well as camping fees. Be prepared to either paddle round the tip of Nootka Island to the surf beach on the other side or have a long carry to the campsite. In summer, the Band usually has someone living in the apartment at the west end of the church and they will take your money and advise you where to camp.

## Friendly Cove

Friendly Cove is the main tourist destination in Nootka Sound. In summer on Wednesdays and Saturdays, the *MV Uchuck* makes a scheduled run here, sometimes bringing busloads of tourists which Mowachaht guides show round the site.

Both legends and archaeologists agree that the Mowachaht have lived at Friendly Cove for over four thousand years. They called it Yuquot—place of many winds. Although Mowachaht means people of the deer, the 4000 people who gathered here each summer were whalers. Using sacred

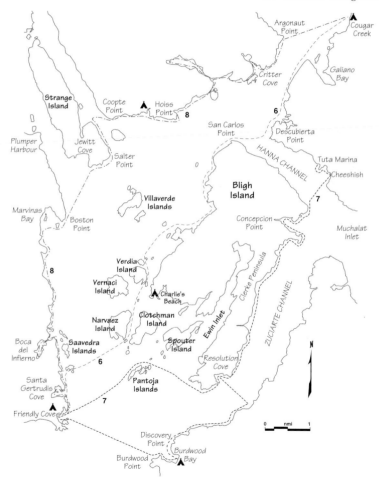

*Friendly Cove lighthouse.*

shrines and rituals they called the whales to their harpoons. The chief and carefully selected men paddled far out into the ocean returning several days later. About once a year, they towed a whale into the cove and a great feast began amidst much pomp and ceremony.

On his third voyage round the world, Captain James Cook became the first European to land in the Pacific Northwest in March 1778. Maquinna welcomed him with gifts of lustrous sea otter furs. After Cook's death in Hawaii, the ships went to Macao where they sold the furs for immense prices. Traders followed.

To discourage the Russians from spreading south from Alaska, the Spanish, who claimed the whole Pacific coast by Papal decree, established a settlement at Friendly Cove. Por-

tuguese, British and American ships arrived a few months later. The Spanish impounded three of them causing a diplomatic fracas in London and Madrid. In 1791, Alejandro Malaspina, on a Spanish scientific expedition round the world, detoured to Friendly Cove to advise and the following year Captain Vancouver and the Spanish Governor, Bodega y Quadra were unable to resolve the differences of their two countries. In 1795, Lt. Thomas Pearce (sometimes spelled Pierce) took possession of Nootka Sound and the Spanish withdrew.

Nothing remains of the Spanish settlement, though in recent years the Spanish government donated two stained glass windows to the Roman Catholic church. These depict Father Catala, chaplain to the Spanish garrison, and the meeting of Vancouver and Quadra. The present church was built in 1954, replacing an earlier one that burned down. It is now a museum containing two sets of glorious house-posts belonging to the Jack and Maquinna families.

The lighthouse, built in 1911, stands on the site of the Spanish fort that welcomed Malaspina, Vancouver and others with 21 gun salutes. After staffing it for almost 34 years, Ed and Pat Kidder retired in May 2003.

In 1967, the Department of Indian Affairs cut off funding for the Friendly Cove school, forcing the now combined Mowachaht/Muchalaht Band members to relocate to a small reserve beside the Gold River pulp mill. One family, Ray and Terry Williams, remained and today are the only permanent residents of Friendly Cove.

In the old days when the Mowachaht governed themselves, there was a platform on the south side of the church down by the edge of the big shingle beach, where they went to resolve disputes. This was called Tutuquis. However long it took, people listened as the two complainants explained their positions and then the elders ruled on the outcome.

At the other end of the outer crescent of shingle, a trail leads past an old graveyard. These are Christian burials complete with headstones or wooden markers. Pass by but do not invade their peace.

Continue on the trail to where a large freshwater lake almost meets the sea. Rental cottages overlook its once sacred waters. The trees in the distance are an island on which a whaler's shrine was revered for hundreds of years until it was stolen

in 1904 and taken to the American Museum of Natural History where it lies in storage boxes. Because of its power, the Band has mixed feelings about having it return. A National Film Board film[5] tells the story.

Back at the main cove, on the north side of the William's house, there are two smaller coves. The first one was often used for guests who were not quite welcome. Maquinna permitted Captain Meares to build the 40 ton *North West America* here. In 1889 Father Augustin Brabant, a Belgian missionary, used the same site to build a Roman Catholic Church. When it burned down in 1954, its replacement, the present church, was built behind the village.

Church window at Friendly Cove depicting meeting of Governor Quadra and Captain Vancouver.

# 7 Tuta Marina to Friendly Cove

**Difficulty** Intermediate conditions – moderate risk
**Distance** 9 nmi one way.
**Duration** 4-5 hours
**Chart** Nootka Sound No. 3675, 1:40,000, depth in metres
**Tides** on Tofino
**Currents** none
**Map** see page 47

Other than taking the *Uchuck*, this is the shortest paddle between a boat launch and Friendly Cove albeit accessed by a rougher road after Cougar Creek. It has the added bonus of visits to Cheeshish and Resolution Cove where Captain Cook anchored his ships for a month in 1778. Friendly Cove is the site of the First Nation's village which he visited and the location of the Spanish settlement

**Paddling considerations:**
- Inflow-outflow winds – especially opposite the mouth of Muchalat Inlet
- Crossings
    - 0.7 nmi
    - Resolution Cove to the beacon below Mt. Adair 0.7 nmi
    - Bligh Island to Friendly Cove 2.7 nmi
    - Burdwood Point to Friendly Cove 2.3 nmi
- Pacific swells affect crossing between Bligh and Burdwood or Friendly Cove
- Surf landing if you go to Burdwood Bay.
- Sea fog

**The route**
From Tuta Marina, paddle east along the coast to the Indian Reserve. Pause a moment. This is the site of Cheeshish, the village where a Muchalat chief gave Captain Cook the cold shoulder, perhaps because Cook had made friends first with the rival Mowachaht. There is nothing there now, but you can think about the incident as you paddle by. One of the daughters of Larry and Shirley Andrews who operate Tuta Marina is the official guardian of Cheeshish.

Cross Hanna Channel to Bligh Island (0.7 nmi) and proceed down its eastern shore on Zuciarte Channel. Just beyond Concepcion Point, a small inlet on Bligh Island opens up. The head of this makes a good place to stop briefly. There are not many others.

Continue along the shore of Clerke Peninsula to Resolution Cove (5 nmi from Tuta Marina). Captain Cook anchored his ships here for a month in 1778. Here, he careened the bottom of one of them and replaced its topmast with a Douglas fir cut from the forest behind. Although his men stepped ashore easily from their longboats, it is more difficult to do this with a kayak as the beach is made up of large rocks about 10 cm and more in

*Harpooner on Maquinna House post in Friendly Cove Church.*

diameter so you can't just run your boat up onto it. Usually there is also a bit of a swell. In fact, it's quite a poor anchorage but Cook didn't know the territory and wanted to be able to put to sea easily if necessary. He prepared to do so when hostile canoes, possibly Muchalaht, came attempting to trade and the Mowachaht under Chief Maquinna chased them away. Even if you don't land, you can probably get close enough to read the inscriptions on the two plaques on the cliff commemorating Cook's visit.

After Resolution Cove, there are two options:

1. Cross Zuciarte Channel (just under 1 nmi) to the flashing red beacon at the foot of Mount Adair and paddle along the shoreline, round Discovery Point and into a large bay with a sandy beach. This is Burdwood Bay. Surfers often camp here on their way to play in the waves of Escalante Beach (3 nmi farther on). Be prepared to do a surf landing here. If it looks daunting, try the south shore of the bay on your right as you paddle in. This may be sheltered from the main force of the surf. There is a creek for water on the left side of the main bay.

Next day, paddle the 2.5 nmi across the entrance to Nootka Sound to Friendly Cove. This crossing is open to the Pacific swells.

2. Continue round the Clerke Peninsula and either cross directly to Friendly Cove (3 nmi subject to open ocean swells) or cross the mouth of Ewing Inlet (1 nmi) into the Spanish Pilot Group of islands.
Small parties may find the odd rocky camp spot here but it will be a bit of a scramble. Many spots that look good on the map but have float houses in them. If the inhabitants arrive, they may party far into the night.

The Spanish Pilot Group are interesting to paddle round but don't expect too many landing places. At low tide, there are lots of colourful purple and orange ochre sea stars and some shell sand coves.

From the southwestern end of the Pantoja Islands, the crossing to Friendly Cove is about 1.7 nmi. Freighters travelling fast on their way to Tahsis used to be a problem when the mill was open. The occasional one may still come in. In August, sea fog often quickly clouds this passage especially at dusk and dawn. Look out to sea before making the crossing to see if it is approaching.

At Friendly Cove, land on the left near the lighthouse and walk up to the Church. Behind it, the Band usually has someone living in the apartment who will take your landing fee and indicate where you may camp. Be prepared to either paddle round the tip of Nootka Island to the surf beach on the other side or have a long carry to the campsite.

# 8 Cougar Creek to Friendly Cove via Hoiss

**Difficulty** Intermediate conditions – moderate risk
**Distance** 12 nmi one way.
**Duration** 6 hours
**Chart** Nootka Sound No. 3675, 1:40,000, depth in metres
**Tides** on Tofino
**Currents** none
**Map** see page 47

This route follows the outer shore of Nootka Sound and pokes into a couple of intriguing coves. Hoiss is a good place to break the journey and camp. After crossing the mouth of Tahsis Inlet, pass Marvinas Bay, the site of the Boston massacre, and follow the coast down to Friendly Cove.

**Paddling considerations:**
- Inflow-outflow winds—you may have to stop at Hoiss.
- Crossings
  – Cougar Creek to Argonaut Point
  – 1.4 nmi
  – Coopte Point to Salter Point on Strange Island 0 .7 nmi. The rocky cove on south side of Strange Island is a surf landing. In case of emergency, try to make it round to Plumper Harbour or Jewitt Cove.
  – Strange Island to Boston Point 1.1 nmi.
- Sea fog at the Friendly Cove end.

**The route**
Cross Tlupana Inlet to Argonaut Point (1.4 nmi) and paddle along the Vancouver Island shore. About one nautical mile along, the pocket cove behind floating Critter Cove Marina is a neat place to poke into. Critter Cove has a small store and restaurant catering

mainly to sport fishers. The owners have been there a long time and know the area and its weather vagaries well. They monitor VHF Channel 6.

The next bay contains a hidden lake at its head. This is only accessible at high tide and is a mosquito haven.

A mile farther on, Hoiss Point is a favourite fishing hole. Beyond it, Hoiss Creek is a good water source. Next to it is a BC Forest Campsite. If the inflow winds are beginning to blow, stop and camp here. There's usually lots of space and sometimes a bear problem so hang food. There are few places to go ashore between here and Friendly Cove.

~

*A warm afternoon wind dumps waves rhythmically on the shingle and chases away the mosquitoes. Chestnut-backed chicadees rustle in the bushes beside me. A distant Steller's jay chatters and kinglets whisper in the upper branches. A raven croaks melodiously. At last, the sun comes out, though between it and the top of Nootka Island lies a thick dark-grey cloud with ragged edges.*

*The steps up to the midden are kept in repair by a group of men who meet once a year to fish and camp here. They also built the kitchen and probably the bench beside the beach fireplace.*

*As evening approaches, the sun stains the white clouds pink and the grey purple. It looks like there will be another clear sunny morning, but that doesn't happen.*

*An overcast sky greets me when I awake. There's no dawn chorus from the birds at Hoiss—just a continuous buzzing of outboard engines as sport fishers head out for Friendly Cove or Beano Creek. A few stop here and patrol up and down Hoiss Point—their voices float disembodied over the water punctuated by occasional whoops as they reel in a big one.*

~

An evening paddle to Coopte Point and the village site beyond it is an option. The site is so steep it looks an unlikely village location. In 1792, José Mariano de Moziño described a colourful coming of age ceremony held there for Maquinna's daughter.[6]

A bit of a detour to Jewitt Cove on Strange Island provides a sheltered place to stop when inflow winds are strong but there's nowhere to pitch a tent. The island was logged in the early nineties but has greened over now.

Strange commanded the expedition which left Dr. John Mackay to spend a winter with the Mowachaht at Friendly Cove in 1786. Jewitt was one of two survivors from the 1802 massacre aboard the trading ship Boston. This massacre happened in Marvinas Bay on the other side of Boston Point. Jewitt's Journal has been republished.[7]

## Friendly Cove Church

The church is now a museum and is well worth visiting. On the way in, notice the two stained glass windows donated by the Spanish government. These depict Vancouver and Quadra meeting and Father Megin Catala talking to the Mowachaht.

Inside the building, which is no longer used for Roman Catholic services, are two sets of house-posts. These are copies of originals belonging to the Maquinna and Jack families. The base figure on one of the Maquinna posts represents a whaler complete with harpoon.

The tops of the Jack posts are a woodpecker and a salmon. The fish refers to a wedding between a Muchalaht bride and a Mowachaht groom. Their grandson, Chief Jerry Jack, told the Royal BC Museum that when the bridal party arrived at the entrance to Friendly Cove, planks were put across the canoes and dancers performed on them. At the same time, ten men dressed as wolves crawled along the shoreline. He thought it must have been quite a sight to see.

The two chiefs had houses with ceilings tall enough to accommodate these posts. Tim Paul and Ki-ke-in carved these full-sized replicas.

*Looking toward Burdwood and Friendly Cove from near Hoiss Point.*

Nootka Fishing Lodge is located a couple of nautical miles south of Boston Point. It is built on the site of an old cannery started by the Everett Packing Company of Washington in 1917. The pilings are still visible. In 1929, Emily Carr, B.C.'s famous artist and a talented writer stayed at the cannery's hotel "...which offended all my five senses."[8]

Using the language of the day, she noted that the different ethnic groups in the thriving community of 75 people liked to remain separate. "Set back among the pines was a great raw frame building. This was where the Norwegians lived. Below them was the little Jap Village neat as a pin with little flowers and green things growing in pots." The Chinese boarding house had "...tatters of derelict curtains hung at the windows and the doors and windows were tight shut."

The hotel was so awful that Carr, moved to the lighthouse.

There is nothing left of an earlier cannery built in 1897 and located a kilometer south in Boca del Infierno. This is a neat place to visit but can only be entered or exited if the narrow tidal race that guards its entrance is in your favour. These reversing tidal rapids are a feature of Santa-Boca Provincial Park which stretches from here along McKay Passage to include Santa Gertrudis Cove.

McKay Passage inside the Saavedra Islands is named after Dr. John Mackay who was the first European to overwinter on the coast (and whose name is spelled at least six ways). Ramón Saavedra was the last commander of the Spanish settlement at Friendly Cove. In those days it was called Santa Cruz de Nutka. It was dismantled and the land turned over to the British in 1795.

Below the Saavedra Islands, which are privately owned, is Santa Gertrudis Cove. From 1898-1927, W.T. Dawley had a store here. Now it's a sheltered boat anchorage but rocky terrain and fallen timber makes the area unsuitable for camping. BC Parks claim there is "a short, rough route to Jewitt Lake from the beach at Santa Gertrudis Cove." Perhaps there is now, but it seemed like impenetrable bush on several occasions when I was there.

~

*The loudest sounds are the waves washing up and down the beach. Grey fish flutter at the water's edge, retreat and flutter again. If I went down there, could I catch them? Perhaps that's what the children in orange life jackets fishing off Ray Williams' dock are catching. Beyond the children, a long row of white gulls define half the length of Ray's 200 foot dock. The sun peeps through a thick grey sky to pick them out. It chased away the sea fog which blanketed the village this morning.*

*From where I sit, serenaded by a song sparrow, the long low arch of the government wharf frames the William's side of the beach. Two white setter dogs guard it all day while their owners fish with Darryl Williams. Behind me a bald eagle laughs artificially. An osprey flies over in search of a meal.*

*Occasional motor boats speed in to land with small batches of tourists who gawk at the fallen totem pole and the church before climbing up the rocky fastness of the lighthouse (visiting hours 8 am-4 pm).*

~

A hundred years of white man's interference with native ways have taken their toll. First the catholic missionaries "freed" the people to wear European style clothes. The men particularly resented pants. Gunboats called bringing booze and terrible tales of what happened when villages displeased them. The missionaries encouraged the building of individual European style houses for each nuclear family, breaking up the discipline of the extended family system and confusing the new generation. Booze became an escape. When imported beer ran out, people brewed spruce beer. Unhappy men terrorized women and children weaker than themselves.

By the time Ed and Pat Kidder arrived to look after the light in 1969, the situation had reached epidemic proportions. One by one families disappeared. People would go away for the weekend and not come back. During their first two years, there were 40 deaths all alcohol related. Soon only the Williams family were left.

# 9 Friendly Cove to Tahsis

**Difficulty** Intermediate conditions – moderate risk
**Distance** 20 nmi one way.
**Duration** 10-12 hours
**Chart** Nootka Sound No. 3675, 1:40,000, depth in metres
**Tides** on Tofino
**Currents** none

Although most paddlers prefer to let the *Uchuck* take them up or down Tahsis Inlet, this trip is an alternative to paddling the outside of Nootka Island. If the two paddlers who drowned in Nuchatlitz Inlet in May 2003 had gone this way, they would be alive today.

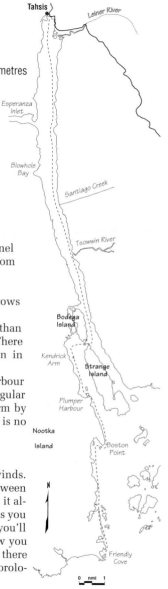

## Paddling considerations

- Inflow winds can be very strong and channel round the points so you can't get away from them.
- Few landing places.
- Possible camp locations: Tsowwin Narrows and Santiago Creek.
- Although more people paddle this inlet than Muchalat, it is also a long, boring paddle. There are more places to scramble ashore than in Muchalat.
- If you want to abort, do so at Plumper Harbour or Kendrick Arm which are both fairly regular *Uchuck* stops on three of its runs. Confirm by calling the ship on VHF Channel 6. There is no bus service to Tahsis.

## The route

Try getting up really early to beat the inflow winds. I've never been successful. Somewhere between Friendly Cove and Boston Point (see Trip 8), it always seems that the inflow winds blow up. As you round each corner, you think that surely now, you'll get some shelter. Nothing doing. They follow you all the way to Plumper Harbour and they're there again when you leave Kendrick Arm. Meteorologists call this channelling.

Both places are *Uchuck* pick-up points. Both are logging camps. A network of roads connects Plumper Harbour with Crawfish Lake in the centre of Nootka Island and Beano Creek where there is now a B&B for hikers of the Nootka Trail. Hikers who find the Nootka Trail too tough may catch a ride here aboard the *Uchuck*. The islands protecting Plumper Harbour are too rocky to camp on and the green looking grass in the cove is sea asparagus which fills with water at high tide so you can't camp there either.

Leaving the shelter of Bodega Island at the north end of Kendrick Arm, test the strength of the wind which can be considerable. The inlet shores are rocky and often impossible to land on should waves begin to build up. One possible shelter is to duck in at the north end of Bodega Island or, if the tide is high, leave Kendrick Arm that way, changing to the Esperanza chart before you do so.

If the weather is reasonable, head up the inlet to Tsowwin Narrows (3 nmi from the south end of Bodega Island), a grassy estuary sticking out into the centre of the inlet.

The wreck marked on the chart between here and Santiago Creek is the Number 2 Ferry which used to run across Burrard Inlet to North Vancouver. Gordon Gibson, a colourful logging personality, who built a sawmill at Tahsis in the forties, bought the ferry for a bunkhouse only it burned within two weeks of arrival.

Santiago Creek is another nautical mile and a half along. Although the chart shows it and the opposite shores as booming grounds, they are little used for this purpose now.

The Blowhole Bay logging camp on the opposite shore is still in use as logging roads from there access the northern end of Nootka Island. Strong cross winds funnel down from the vee in the mountains causing grief to many small boaters.

One and a half nautical miles north of Blowhole Bay and on the same side, the channel opens to the left. This is the head of Esperanza Inlet (Trip 10).

Tahsis is 3 nmi farther. West Bay Park, on the left a short distance before the boat launch, has some picnic sites down by the water and possibly some room for camping up the hill. Otherwise try the open grassy area at the head of the inlet in front of the restaurant.

Often paddlers put in at Tahsis to paddle Esperanza Inlet to Catala and Nuchatlitz, a long day's paddle away.

Tahsis is a small community which was once sustained by a thriving sawmill built by Gordon Gibson in 1947. Its legendary rainfall, which averages 5000 mm (200 inches) a year caused many workers to arrive on one steamship and leave on the next. There are a couple of grocery stores, a liquor outlet and a restaurant but no bank or bus service.

Before the Europeans came, Tahsis was Maquinna's main winter village. From here, a native trading route exported strings of shell money, canoes and slaves to the Kwakwaka'-wakw people near Alert Bay. On the way back, they brought precious boxes of oolichan grease, an essential condiment in the Mowachaht diet.

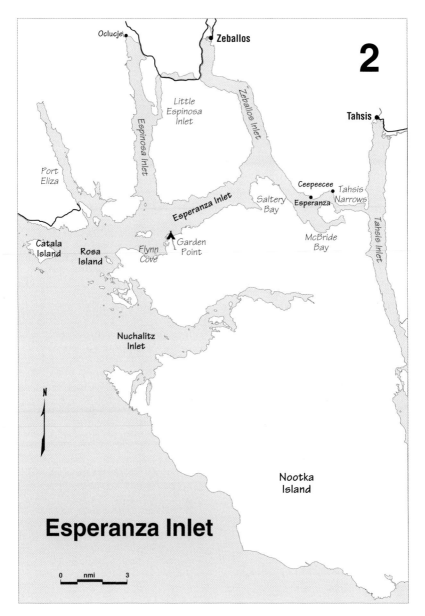

Oclucje

Zeballos

**2**

*Little Espinosa Inlet*

*Espinosa Inlet*

*Zeballos Inlet*

**Tahsis**

*Port Eliza*

*Esperanza Inlet*

Ceepeecee
*Tahsis Narrows*

*Saltery Bay*

Esperanza

*Tahsis Inlet*

*McBride Bay*

**Catala Island**

**Rosa Island**

*Flynn Cove*

*Garden Point*

**Nuchalitz Inlet**

**Nootka Island**

N

# Esperanza Inlet

0    nmi    3

Esperanza Inlet is the gateway to Nuchatlitz, Catala, and the outside of Nootka Island, all wonderful paddling areas. Locations of historical interest in Esperanza are Ehatisaht, Flynn Cove, and Queen Cove.

Captain Cook initially tried to make landfall here but was afraid to bring his ships in among the spray covered rocks. He called it the Bay of Hope and the Spaniards translated the name to Esperanza.

Esperanza is a long inlet connected to Tahsis Inlet, and therefore Nootka Sound, by a narrow gap at its head. From there it opens out into the sheltered areas of Tahsis Narrows, Ceepeecee and McBride Bay before reaching Hecate Channel and the main inlet. The top extension of Hecate Channel is Zeballos Inlet and farther down two more branches enter the north side of main inlet. These are Espinosa Inlet and Port Eliza.

There are few human settlements on these inlets. The Esperanza Mission opposite McBride Bay runs Christian retreats. Zeballos had a mini gold rush in the 1930s and still hangs in there with tourism and some fishing and forestry. Several fish farms producing Atlantic salmon have opened up where Zeballos Inlet meets Hecate Channel and there's another up Port Eliza. After 1968, when the road connected Zeballos and Fair Harbour (on Kyuquot Sound) to the rest of Vancouver Island, the Department of Indian Affairs transferred the First Nations people from Nuchatlitz to Oclucje at the head of Espinosa Inlet and from Ehatisaht to Zeballos.

### Fish Farms – Two Views

Grieg Seafood B.C. Ltd is a family owned company operating six sea farms near Zeballos. It is committed to long-term sustainable aquaculture and helped sponsor the on-land rearing experiment near Nanaimo. A company spokesperson says: "Atlantics do a better job of converting feed to flesh," and the selling price is higher than for Pacific stocks. The Pacific Surveyor, a vessel operated by a third party reporting directly to the federal and provincial governments, monitors the seabed around Grieg's farms. In 2002, these farms had "minimal impact on the surrounding seabed environment" and no fish escapes. See also www.salmonfarmers.org.

The Suzuki Foundation's Otto Langer notes that waste discharged into the water from net-pen sea farms brings disease to the marine environment, even if farm sites are rotated. Federal and provincial governments have promoted the industry without regulating it properly. Cheap farmed salmon have depressed the market for wild salmon putting local fishers out of work. He cites studies showing that escaped Atlantic salmon are now competing with Pacific stocks for spawning rivers and that salmon farms enhance sea lice populations which have devastated the pink salmon population in Johnstone Strait. See also www.davidsuzuki.org/files/Oceans/March030technicalpaper.

With several road access points, some paddlers do round trips shuttling vehicles between put-in and take-out points. Some popular ones are:

- Zeballos to Little Espinosa Inlet. Hitchhike or walk the 7.6 km between them.
- Little Espinosa, round Tatchu Point to Fair Harbour. The shoals and reefs off Tatchu mean that paddlers have to go a mile or more offshore in exposed lumpy water. Only experienced paddlers should attempt this—and be prepared to turn back.
- Tahsis, Zeballos or Little Espinosa, down the outside of Nootka Island to Friendly Cove and then back up Tahsis Inlet. This is also an advanced trip. Paddlers should be proficient at surf landings and be prepared to divert to the inside. Two paddlers drowned in 2003 attempting the outside of Nootka Island during bad weather.

The *MV Uchuck* also provides launching anywhere and pick-up at specific points. This can add to the permutations and combinations. As their schedule is subject to last minute changes, when on the water waiting for pick-up, call them on VHF Channel 6 for an estimated time of arrival. You'll only get through if you are within line of sight.

### Launches

### Tahsis, Tahsis Inlet

From Gold River, follow the signs for Tahsis. Pavement ends in about 2 kilometres. Cross the Gold River, and turn left. Cross another bridge and turn right up a hill. This is the Tahsis road. It is well maintained and well used.

At fifty-seven kilometers, watch for a big Douglas fir tree on the right-hand side of the road. This is the President's Tree, a landmark beloved by Tahsis residents who know that they are nearing home when they pass it. The tree is named after Jack Christiansen, former president of Tahsis Company, who, when the road was being built, decreed that a sample big fir should be left.

Farther on, the green moss of the old-growth forest drenches the BC Forest campsite on the Leiner River and mutes the traffic noise from the road. Campers here are lulled to sleep by the river chuckling past their tents all night.

To reach the boat launch, follow the main road round the head of the Inlet and through the town. Eventually, it comes down to a former hotel and some empty stores. The boat launch is just beyond

### Zeballos, Zeballos Inlet

The village of Zeballos is 40 km down a well-used logging road which leaves the Island Highway (No.19) a short distance north of Woss. The turnoff is well signed. The same road goes to Fair Harbour which is 36 km beyond Zeballos. Two kilometres in, there is a right turn-off to the Hustan Caves and another at 8 km to Atluk Lake and the Artlish Road. Stay on the main road.

At 38 km the road divides with the right fork continuing to Fair Harbour and the left fork leading 4 km directly into Zeballos. Drive right through town, past the museum and the hotel. The boat launch is on the left just before the store and gas pump.

*Espinosa Inlet from Oclucje.*

Water taxi services from Zeballos will take kayaks to places within the inlets. For phone numbers, check the signs on the road into Zeballos (see page 163).

### Resolution Park, Zeballos Inlet
Just outside Zeballos on the Fair Harbour road is the new home of the Ehattesaht Band who formerly lived on Esperanza Inlet. Hefty speed bumps slow vehicles to a crawl. After this the road climbs around a log sorting area and provides good views over Zeballos Inlet. As the road turns west, a 4WD road on the left heads to Resolution Park. Launching from there cuts off 1 nmi of paddling which could be critical in the morning if trying to reach Garden Point before the wind comes up—but 4WD is a neces-

sity. It has a cobble beach which can be tough to haul gear over at low tide. Parked vehicles are safer left by the Zeballos wharf. If morning tides are low, consider overnighting at Zeballos and rising earlier.

### Little Espinosa Inlet
Follow the directions for Resolution Park but continue on. One kilometre along the Fair Harbour road the top half of Little Espinosa Inlet is glimpsed on the right. The road runs above it before descending to a wooden bridge between the two halves. Because it is tidal, this narrow passage periodically becomes a raging torrent of whitewater with a 1 m drop. Launch on the outer side of the bridge. On occasion, vehicles have been vandalised here. Alternately, drive the

vehicles back to Zeballos and walk, hitch-hike or taxi the 7.6 km back.

## Oclucje, Espinosa Inlet

Four kilometres beyond the Little Espinosa bridge, there is a turn-off to Oclucje (pronounced Ook-la-gee). This hamlet of about five houses is the home of the Nuchatlitz Indian Band who moved here from their island village at the mouth of Esperanza Inlet in 1987. Oclucje, less than five minutes along this side road, looks directly down to the mouth of Espinosa Inlet. A dock below the village has a boat launching ramp beside it. Those who launch here should first make arrangements with the villagers for permission and parking. If there's no one to talk to, return to Little Espinosa.

### *MV Uchuck* – see Gold River

The *Uchuck* overnights at Zeballos on Mondays and at Kyuquot on Thursdays.

## Camping Locations

### Zeballos

The municipal RV campground is on the river. If this is full, drive to the boat launch, pack the boats and paddle down to Resolution Park.

### Resolution Park (Previously called Rhodes Creek Park)

This BC Forest Service campsite has seven units. Driving down hill to the waterside park is easy but getting back up without four-wheel drive may be impossible. The site has water. Consider launching at Zeballos and paddling over the night before attempting the inlet.

*Kayakers arriving at Garden Point.*

*Zeballos Museum.*

**Lord Waterfall** on Lutes Creek on the east side of Hecate Channel. A short recreation trail along an old logging road leads to a waterfall. Esperanza Mission suggest camping here or at Haven Cove during July when they are busy. Both spots are tiny.

**Haven Cove**, on the west side of Hecate Channel. Room for one tent, maybe. This site and Lord Waterfall are marked on several maps as camp-sites despite their minuscule size.

**Esperanza**
Ask permission at the office before camping and give a donation to the Nootka Mission. In July, only emergency camping is permitted as children's camps are in session.

**Garden Point**
This BC Forest Service campsite among the old-growth trees above a sandy beach is the most beautiful campsite on Esperanza, but bears have been a repeated problem. Hang food at all times. They know how to pop kayak hatches and that plastic containers contain food. Fresh water is available from nearby Brodick Creek but make sure you go far enough upstream to leave the salt water behind.

**Rosa Island** see Section 3, Nuchatlitz.

**Catala Island** see Section 4 Catala Island

# 10 Tahsis to Esperanza

**Difficulty** Intermediate conditions – moderate risk
**Distance** 6 nmi one way.
**Duration** 2-2 1/2 hours
**Chart** Esperanza Inlet No. 3676, 1: 40,000, depth in metres
**Tides** on Tofino
**Currents** none

Although some people paddle in from Tahsis, this is a less popular route for accessing Esperanza Inlet than putting in at Zeballos or Little Espinosa. Those who really want to see Esperanza and Ceepeecee can easily reach them from Zeballos.

**Paddling considerations:**
• Inflow-outflow winds in Tahsis Inlet
• Crossings: none

**The route**
From the boat launch at Tahsis, paddle 3 nmi down Tahsis Inlet and turn west round Mozino Point and into Tahsis Narrows. This is the most sheltered water of the whole trip and often good fishing which is why Steamer Point Lodge was built just beyond its western entrance. The Lodge is on the site of the first aid station for the defunct Ceepeecee Cannery. CPC stood for the California

Packing Corporation which built a pilchard cannery in 1926. The pilchards disappeared in the early 1940s. The cannery, which by this time also canned salmon, limped along until its owners shut it down in 1951. Three years later fire burned much of it. The remains are a boat yard where yachts and small power boats can be taken out of the water for repairs.

The small white cottage below Steamer Point Lodge is of historic sig-

## Esperanza Mission

In 1937, Percy Wills, the sole Vancouver Island missionary for the Shantymen's Christian Association, persuaded Dr. Herman McLean to open a hospital at Esperanza on a sunny, level bench often used by the native people. It was the first hospital north of Tofino. Although never funded well enough to meet provincial standards, many would have died without it.

Over the years, the building was enlarged several times and separate houses added for the McLean family and the staff. Within a few metres of the hospital, the government allowed a hotel to be built whose beer parlour was frequently patronised by boisterous Ceepeecee cannery workers. Much to the McLean's relief it burnt down in 1960 and the mission built the present dining room on the site.

The hospital's motto was "To Preach Christ and Heal Diseases." Patients' souls were as important as their bodies. While many welcomed this approach, some did not. In 1950, Zeballos built a hospital that operated without a religious emphasis. Unfortunately, it also placed native people of both sexes in the same ward, which upset them. Not surprisingly, most continued to choose Esperanza. They knew Dr. McLean from his regular visits to their villages at Nuchatlitz, Queen Cove, and Kyuquot and to the many logging camps that dotted the inlets.

Dr. McLean retired in 1972 and died three years later. The hospital closed in 1973. However others, notably Earl and Louise Johnson, continued the missionary work. For three years the Mission used the Esperanza facilities to operate a dental clinic. They also ran a school for native children and a summer camp for them at Camp Ferrier[11] on Louie Bay Nuchatlitz Inlet.

nificance. It belonged to John and Pete Perry, two brothers who first settled at the head of Tahsis Inlet at the mouth of the Leiner River. When Gordon Gibson built his sawmill across the inlet from them, they moved the house to this quieter location. The brothers, who originally lived at Friendly Cove, were of Latvian origin and were great photographers. Their pictures now reside in the BC Archives. Even this new location was too busy for them so they retired to Osoyoos in the interior of the province.

### Esperanza

The Nootka Mission at Esperanza provides counselling programs for families suffering alcohol and drug abuse as well as hosting church and health groups for retreats. This service is all that remains of the legacy of Dr. Herman McLean who ran a medical practice here beginning in 1937. Today only a concrete pad shows where the hospital stood as the building became unsafe and had to be demolished in 1991.

Passing boaters often call at the gas dock where a small store sells junk food and bait. Visitors are welcome to go ashore except in July when the Mission operates a children's camp. On landing, check with the staff before unloading and give a donation to the Mission.

# 11 Zeballos to Ehatisaht

**Difficulty** Intermediate – moderate risk
**Distance** 8 nmi one way.
Duration 3-4 hours
**Chart** Esperanza Inlet No. 3676, 1: 40,000, depth in metres
**Tides** on Tofino
**Currents** none

This paddle is best done early in the day to get as far as possible down Esperanza Inlet before the wind gets up. Watch for wildlife as you go.

## Paddling considerations
- Inflow-outflow winds
- Crossings: none
- Scarce landings

## The route

If morning tides are high, camp at Resolution Park for an early start. The islands where the inlet bends to the south are prettily ornamented with shore pines. Leave the exploration of the estuary of the Little Zeballos River on the other side of the inlet for the return journey. Overgrown logging debris makes it hard to move around on shore and you need to make time down Esperanza Inlet before the wind comes up.

Past the islands much of the shore is cliffs so keep snacks reachable while in the boats. The remains of a few old cabins stick out of the bush occasionally and if you're lucky a bear or two will be around.

Ehatisaht was the village where Maquinna brought John Jewitt, the survivor of the Boston massacre, to marry the chief's daughter. After the ceremony, they returned to Maquinna's winter village at Tahsis but were not allowed to see each other for ten days.

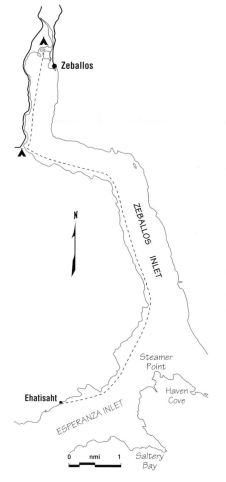

*The modern Zeballos Hotel.*

Here, also, stood one of the last totem poles on this coast. Sometimes called the Queen Mary pole, it was raised in 1912 in honour of Mary Jack, wife of Captain Jack of Friendly Cove. In 1985, it was loaded on the *Uchuck* and sent to the Provincial Museum in Victoria. A replica, carved by Tim Paul, whose mother is buried at Ehatisaht, was erected in Zeballos in 1988 but blew down within weeks amidst much controversy. The elders wanted it erected at Ehatisaht and objected to the Zeballos location while the younger members of the band wanted it to be at Zeballos so that they could have houses built there. They won and their houses are just out of Zeballos on the road to Fair Harbour.

### Zeballos

Zeballos was named after Ciriaco de Cevallos, a lieutenant in the Spanish Navy. He and Lt. José Espinosa explored the area by launch in August 1791 under orders from Alejandro Malaspina who had arrived at Friendly Cove on a scientific expedition.

In 1924, Quatsino prospectors found gold in the river and a vein which they staked. Others followed and over six million dollars worth of gold came out of the White Star, Privateer and other mines in the area. Zeballos' population swelled to a thousand. Laurel & Hardy played at the Community Hall which opened with a masked ball on Halloween night in 1938. There was even a bordello.

The gold mines became uneconomic and shut down in 1948 when the government pegged the price at $35 an ounce.

# 12 Ehatisaht to Catala Island (North side of Esperanza Inlet)

**Difficulty** Intermediate conditions – moderate risk
**Distance** 8 nmi one way.
**Duration** 3-4 hours
**Chart** Esperanza Inlet No. 3676, 1: 40,000, depth in metres
**Tides** on Tofino
**Currents** none

The route gets more interesting as you go along past the entrance to Espinosa Inlet, with sea caves in the pink cliffs, the entrance to Port Eliza and a glimpse of Queen Cove with its old church before a short hop across Rolling Roadstead to Catala Island. This side of the inlet has fewer places to land than the south side but saves what can be a dangerous crossing.

## Paddling considerations
- Inflow-outflow winds make Esperanza hazardous to cross after they blow up. Don't try it after 10 am.
- In an emergency, the east end of Graveyard Bay is a possibility for a couple of tents. Don't try the village of Ehatisaht as it is a graveyard and local fishing vessels, which patrol the inlet, will land and you will be asked to leave.
- Crossings
  – The mouth of Espinosa Inlet to Otter Island 0.8 nmi
  – Birthday Channel at its narrowest point 0.2 nmi
  – Southern tip of Harbour Island to the mainland 0.5 nmi.
  – Mainland to Catala across Rolling Roadstead 0.5 nmi
- Sea fog. Set compass courses before leaving.

## The route
Although the siren-like beauty of Garden Point on the opposite side of the inlet may beckon, stay on this side unless it's a flat calm day. There's no camping at Ehatisaht but, provided

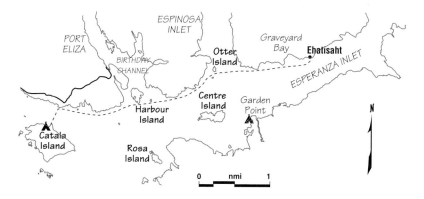

the tide doesn't come up too high, there is space for two tents at the east end of Graveyard Bay which is the next one down the inlet. At the west end of the bay, Bill Smith's grave used to have a wooden cross but the undergrowth has buried it.

Look north up Espinosa Inlet. The tiny white houses at the end belong to Oclucje, the village to which the Nuchatlitz people moved. Newton Cove is on the west side of the entrance to Espinosa Inlet.

Past Otter Island, watch for sea caves in the pink cliffs. If the water is calm, it's fun to poke the boats into these but watch the surge. Crossing Birthday Channel, keep an eye out for wind and tide funnelling out of Port Eliza and be prepared to ferry glide across the short distance.

On the way over, the village of Queen Cove comes into view on the right. The tiny church on the hill is one of the few remaining churches built by Father Augustin Brabant, a Belgian Roman Catholic Priest, who hitchhiked around the coast "in the days when the protestants were scared to."

Follow the coast, if necessary filling up with water from one of the creeks on the mainland as there is none on Catala Island. Double Island is rocky and not a good landing though some years ago kayakers in distress scrambled ashore and called a passing fish boat for help. They were lucky there was one.

If Rolling Roadstead is acting up to its name, camp on the mainland

*Grave in Graveyard Bay.*

or wait until either a tide change or dusk when the water may calm long enough for the crossing.

Opposite the triangular spit on Catala, cross over. This spit has a surge on it. Check both sides to see which is easier to land on and be prepared to be quick. Send in the most skilled paddler first and then the rest. Have carrying straps ready and, leaving one person to mind the boats, heave the rest up on top of the shingle as fast as possible. For further details see Section 4, Catala Island

# 13  Little Espinosa and Espinosa Inlet to Esperanza Inlet

**Difficulty**  Intermediate conditions – moderate risk.
**Distance**  5.5 nmi one way.
**Duration**  2-3 hours
**Chart**  Esperanza Inlet No. 3676, 1: 40,000, depth in metres
**Tides**  on Tofino
**Currents**  none

Little Espinosa is a delightful sheltered waterway to start out on.

### Paddling considerations
- Inflow-outflow winds
- Crossings
  – Eastern shore of Espinosa Inlet to
  Otter Island 0.7 nmi
  – From Espinosa to Garden Point
  1.5 nmi
- Sea fog in Esperanza Inlet. Set com-
  pass courses before leaving.

### The route
Linger in Little Espinosa on the way
back, not on the way out. Have a
short break on the beach where Little
Espinosa joins its wider parent. Coming out into Espinosa Inlet itself, look
northwards for a glimpse of Oclucje,
the village to which the Nuchatlitz
people moved on the mainland.

Half way to the mouth of Espinosa
an old log dump is a less scenic place
to stop. There's not much else. Newton Cove on the opposite side is also a
possible picnic spot but read the sidebar on page 72 before camping there!

At the mouth of Espinosa, either
cross Esperanza to Garden Point or
stay on the north side of the inlet and
continue on to Catala (see Trip 12).

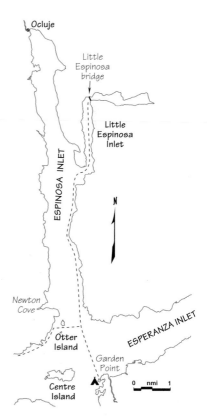

*Espinosa Inlet from Oclucje.*

## Don't Camp On Sea Asparagus!

Four of us -- Bud, Ray, Lorne and myself, being new to the West Coast, got up late and launched at Little Espinosa about 11am. By the time we reached the entrance to Esperanza Inlet a wind had got up which made it impossible to cross.

Instead, we camped at Newton Cove which has no comfortable place to pitch a tent. Bud was wise and, after first pitching his in a streambed, moved it to a rocky outcrop above the vegetation and promptly fell fast asleep missing all the later excitement. Though at least two of the rest should have known better, we ignored the warning of the sea asparagus plant which grows on the high tide line and made camp on top of it at the edge of the shingle.

Exhausted, I went to sleep about 9.30 p.m. Half an hour later, Lorne's voice outside said, "You better get up, the tide's within three inches of your tent and it's got another two hours to come up." Hastily we repitched the two tents on the rocky shore just below the sleeping Bud. At 11 o'clock, the voice came again: "I'm floating and you probably are too." I was.

Stumbling around in the dark, we re-pitched Ray's tent on the only other place -- on top of the stream bed where Bud's had originally been. In the morning, my abandoned tent had 30cm of water in it. We've never ignored sea asparagus since.

## Garden Point Bear Problems

In 2000, two women had no problems till they began to cook breakfast. The bear padded purposefully toward them and they were unable to continue. One woman paddled out to a power boat anchored in the bay. The U.S. owner gave her a lecture about why she should be carrying fire arms but came ashore and warned the bear off with a few shots. After breakfast while they were packing up to leave, the bear returned and refused to leave. Again the woman had to summon the power boat operator. Neither of them appreciated this.

*Garden Point Beach.*

# 14 Esperanza to Steamer Point to Rosa Island (South side of Esperanza Inlet)

**Difficulty** Intermediate conditions – moderate risk
**Distance** 11.5 nmi one way.
**Duration** 3-5 hours
**Chart** Esperanza Inlet No. 3676, 1: 40,000, depth in metres
**Tides** on Tofino
**Currents** none

Although winds can kick up nasty waves on Esperanza Inlet, there are lots of places to land on the south side; more so than on the north.

## Paddling considerations

- Inflow-outflow winds on Esperanza Inlet are strong. Plan to reach Garden Point before 10 am and possibly wait until evening before proceeding further.
- Crossings
  – Esperanza to the west side of Hecate Channel 0.7 nmi
  – Saltery Bay 0.6 nmi
- Sea fog toward Rosa Island.

## The route

From Esperanza, cross Hecate Channel at the mouth of McBride Bay and remain on that side.

Haven Cove, also known as God's Pocket, is a pretty place to stop. If you scramble up the hill and look back at the trunks of the cedar trees, you may find some that have had strips of bark removed. These are known as CMTs—Culturally Modified Trees. In the old days, First Nation's women used the bark to make baskets and waterproof cedar capes and hats.

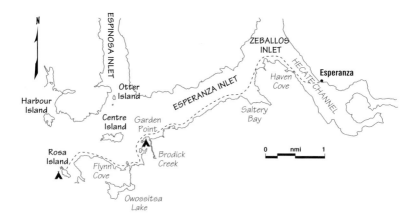

*Caroline Stoddart being launched from the Uchuck at Rosa Island.*

Past the fish farm which rears Atlantic salmon, round Steamer Point and the main part of Esperanza Inlet opens up in front of you. There are several nice beaches and a logging camp just before Brodick Creek which may not be operational.

Garden Point is a beautiful BC Forest campsite reminiscent of the tropics. Wade up the river till it loses its salty flavour, fill up water containers, do the laundry and indulge in a hair washing session. If you plan to camp here, keep your food hung well out of the reach of the several bears which patrol the area. There's more than one

and they know that plastic containers produce food and even how to take off a kayak hatch.

Centre Island in the bay beyond Garden Point is very rocky and almost impossible to land on. Besides, the owner does not welcome uninvited visitors. Instead, follow the coast. In the bay there are several coves with cabins in them. Sometimes the owners are there, sometimes not. One has left a note saying guests are welcome provided they leave everything the way they found it.

Owossitsa Creek is a gem not to be missed. Paddle alongside the midden and up the creek the short distance that it will let you. It's a tranquil hidden world of Pacific rainforest jungle.

Continuing round the bay, the last cove is protected by a couple of islands. In behind is a very special place, Flynn Cove. Land and ask at the house for permission to hike up to Owossitsa Lake. The half-hour hike is a welcome change from days of paddling. Recently the road has been extended down to the lake where the Gumpoldsbergers keep a canoe for their guests. The lake is quite large with several islands and would be a good place to explore on a day when the wind is up.

Leaving Flynn Cove, watch for a cave part-way along to the point opposite Rosa Island. On calm days, kayaks can paddle into it but watch the surge. There's also a narrow pocket beach for a lunch stop but its strong surge makes landing and re-launching tricky.

Round the last point, a bay opens up in the lee of Rosa Island. This is where the *Uchuck* launches and picks up kayakers heading for the Nuchatlitz Islands.

## Flynn Cove

In 1914 Stan Newton and his wife built a log cabin and ran the first post office in the area from 1919 until 1942. Stan's brother, Gordon, homesteaded on the other side of the cove and eventually sold to Dr. McLean of Esperanza who built a summer home there. Its foundations are still visible.

In 1956, a flying veterinarian from Seattle and his wife, Wally and Bethine Flynn, bought the cove and the surrounding 239 acres. They used their yellow pigeon plane to commute between their Seattle and Alaskan veterinary practices. Later they retired to what by this time was called Flynn Cove and Bethine wrote two books about their adventures.[10]

Bethine Flynn continued to spend summers at the cabin until the road between Tahsis and Gold River was built in 1972. The next winter, thieves ransacked and torched the cabin. For years the place remained an empty ruin. Then in the 1993, Flynn sold to Josef and Ann Gumpoldsberger. Being young and vigorous, they have rebuilt the cabin, added two more where the road turns up to Owossitsa Lake, cleared the road and are now building a large house overlooking the Cove. They plan to offer B&B especially to weary kayakers. For details, see contacts on page 163.

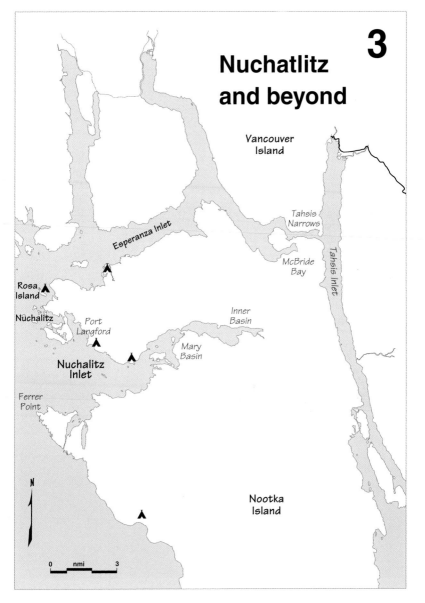

# 3

# Nuchatlitz
# and beyond

Vancouver
Island

Tahsis
Narrows

Esperanza Inlet

McBride
Bay

Tahsis Inlet

Rosa
Island

Nuchalitz

Port
Langford

Inner
Basin

Mary
Basin

Nuchalitz
Inlet

Ferrer
Point

N

Nootka
Island

0    nmi    3

Nuchatlitz is one of the most scenic areas of the west coast. Its many tiny islets and rocky skerries are a kayaker's delight. Beaches of white sand or fine pebbles punctuate the rocky shores. A resident population of sea otters hang around disporting themselves in the kelp beds. There are a number of large sea caves including a spouting cave. Low tide reveals a colourful world of invertebrates: sea stars ranging from pink through purple to bright orange and scarlet; crabs which decorate their shells as a disguise; green, pink, brown and scarlet anemones; and orange cup corals and purple sponges.

The Nuchatlitz Provincial Park consists of 2135 hectares of rocky islands forming relatively protected waterways between Rosa Island and Port Langford. As long as they keep an eye on the wind patterns and stay within the islands, relatively inexperienced paddlers can enjoy the area.

As this place is so popular, don't expect a wilderness experience, especially as it is highly likely that several groups will be competing for the same small camp spots. Share graciously and make new friends. Some people set up camp and do day trips or just hang out.

The only places suitable for large groups are 1-2 hours paddle away at Belmont and Benson Points. Guided groups, which now have to be licenced to use certain areas, do not have exclusive use of them. Hopefully, they will confine themselves to these camp spots.

The Nuchatlitz Band sometimes has members living on the reserve. They like their privacy and so do the bears who come every day to eat blackberries.

*Sunset at Benson Beach.*

*Belmont Beach.*

Behind the Reserve, another island was purchased by a consortium from Los Angeles and subdivided for cottages many of which are owned by residents of the Courtenay area on Vancouver Island.

For water, stock up at Garden Point, Port Langford, Bellmont, Benson or Guise Creek in Mary Basin. There is a limited water supply at Nuchatlitz but first ask permission of either of the De Vault cousins. There is no guarantee of the water's quality.

The lagoons behind the cottages are sheltered places to explore when the wind is too strong to paddle elsewhere. At low tide, you won't be able to get into the farthest one but you'll see dark blue and red bat stars in the shallow water at the entrance. On a high tide, beach the boats on the south-east side and bushwhack through to Port Langford. From there, hike a couple of shingle beaches to Grassy Knoll overlooking Nuchatlitz Inlet.

Nuchatlitz Inlet has more of the same and also some beautiful sandy beaches at Belmont, Benson and Tongue points. From the lagoon at Tongue Point, a hike through old growth forest leads to Third Beach on the outside of Nootka Island.

The outside of Nootka Island has wonderful sandy beaches with surf landings.

## Launches

The *MV Uchuck* travels down Esperanza Inlet on Thursdays, overnights in Kyuquot and returns on Fridays. It can drop kayaks and canoes anywhere but pick-up is at designated points such as Rosa Island, Port Eliza, Ceepeecee etc. See Esperanza Inlet.

## Camping Locations

### Rosa Island
On the east end of the island, behind a small sandy beach, there's a fairly extensive camping area in the forest. BC Parks have equipped it with a green plastic pit toilet. Paddlers often congregate here when the *Uchuck* is expected so you may have to share with others.

There are a few small campsites on other islands nearby. Find your own and be prepared to share. In the summer there are sometimes more campers than sites.

### Belmont Point on the east side of the mouth of Port Langford.
This big terraced meadow is guarded by a surf beach. Water is available from a nearby stream.

### Benson Point on the north west entrance to Mary Basin has a superb sandy beach.
Landing is easiest on the inner beach which still has some surge. The sunsets are wonderful, but as night draws on the sand fleas can be a problem if your tent lacks mosquito netting. Bears patrol the beach at low tide looking for gourmet crustaceans on the rocky islets. Live and let live. Look for wolf and cougar tracks near the waterfall at the west end.

*From inside a sea cave on the way to Benson Point.*

**Tongue Point** at the entrance to Louie Bay on the south side of Nuchatlitz Inlet. Land on the inside of the bay before the blown-up remains of a metal freighter. Behind the small grassy meadow an overgrown trail leads up to Camp Ferrier where Esperanza used to operate a children's summer camp. At night, listen for wolf howls.

**Calvin Creek** half-way down the outside of Nootka Island requires a surf landing, but has a beautiful beach and a waterfall.

**Beano Creek**, half-way between Calvin Creek and Bajo Point on the outside of Nootka Island, requires a surf landing. The beach is fine gravel not sand.

# 15 Rosa Island to Grassy Knoll

**Difficulty** Beginner conditions – low risk
**Distance** 3 nmi one way.
**Duration** 1-2 hours
**Chart** Esperanza Inlet No. 3676, 1: 40,000, depth in metres
**Tides** on Tofino
**Currents** none

This trip is great to examine low tide creatures but if you don't want to portage the shallows between the mainland and the first and third islands, wait for midtide. The three islands bordering Nuchatlitz Inlet each have their own charms: black oystercatchers nest on the first one, the second has a burial cave and the third sandy beaches, an old wrecked barge and a spouting cave. Opposite it, Grassy Knoll gives a superb view.

## Paddling considerations
- Inflow-outflow winds
- Crossings: minimal between the islands
- Often no boats are close enough to help
- Could be paddled in fog by following the shoreline.

## The route
From Rosa Island, head south through the islands keeping on the inside of the outer ones. There's an area of rocky islets fringed with giant kelp fronds. Look for decorator crabs on the fronds. Distant mop heads either turn into bull kelp or sea otters and half a mile offshore there are likely to be rafts of 40-50 of them. Watch the weather if you venture that far out.

Three islands border Nuchatlitz Inlet. If you land on the first one, be careful not to disturb the black oystercatchers. They lay their eggs on the shingle often beside bleached limpet shells and they are so well disguised that even if you photograph them, it's hard to find the egg in the picture afterwards. The more the birds call, the closer you are to the nest and the more reason to leave.

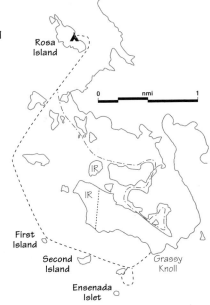

## Stabbers or Hammerers?

Oystercatchers eat more than oysters. Their diet consists of marine invertebrates especially mussels, worms and sea urchins, fish, crustaceans, barnacles, limpets, shrimp. They have two methods of opening a bivalve with their long stout beaks which are strengthened by being triangular in cross section.

Adults teach the young to sneak up on an open mollusc, then stab their beak between the shells and sever the adductor muscles which normally hold the two halves together. They then clean out the contents. Although molluscs often sit with their shells slightly ajar, sometimes, it takes the young birds two years to perfect the technique.

The second method is to detach the shell from the rock it is attached to and then hammer at one side till it breaks and they can get at the contents.

The burial cave on the second island should be left undisturbed. Look but do not touch. There is a heavy fine for disturbing objects on heritage sites like this. Were these people buried here to warn the main village when 10 metre Haida canoes swept down from the north in search of slaves and other plunder? The view from the cave looks far up the coast almost to the Brooks Peninsula. When they saw the Haida coming did the ghosts slip over to the village and warn the people? Perhaps they signalled to the sentries on top of Grassy Knoll. Then a warrior would slip quickly down the back of it, run along the beach and along the trail to the inner lagoon. Concealed from the ocean invaders, he'd paddle like mad for the village.

The third island has a surf beach on the inside. To avoid this go around on the east side, past the spouting cave to the sheltered lagoon behind Ensenada Islet and land on the fine white shell beach. On no account attempt to enter the lagoon from the west side. A concealed rock garden guards it except on the calmest of days.

*Exploring sea cave on Third Island.*

*Nuchatlitz Inlet from Grassy Knoll.*

**Tsunamis**

Drill cores taken from the lake on Catala Island showed evidence of a tsunami which occurred on 26 January 1700. Rising sea levels from such a tsunami, which was caused by a magnitude 9 earthquake in the Cascadia subduction zone, were estimated to be five metres on the coast and up to 15-20 metres at the heads of the inlets.[1] Tsunamis move at speeds near 400 knots. In 1964, one came up sheltered Zeballos Inlet and turned the community hall around.

Walk back to the first beach (50 metres) and scramble over the cliff to the big cave whose entrance is visible from the water. This island is a great place to spend a sunny afternoon but if the wind comes up followed by a high tide, the beach disappears and there is no room to camp.

Opposite on the mainland of Nootka Island, the hummock the locals call Grassy Knoll is obvious. Land on the west side and climb up the trail. The view over Nuchatlitz Inlet and Mary Basin is stupendous. On a clear day, you can see south to Ferrer Point and north to the Brooks Peninsula. Dark orange Indian paintbrush, pink nodding onion, white oxeye daisies and cow parsnip make a beautiful flower garden. As an added bonus the cove on the inner side has the warmest water of anywhere in the islands. Great for swimming!

# 16 Rosa Island to Nuchatlitz lagoons

**Difficulty** Novice conditions – minimal risk
**Distance** 2.5 nmi one way.
**Duration** 1-2 hours
**Chart** Esperanza Inlet No. 3676, 1: 40,000, depth in metres
**Tides** on Tofino
**Currents** none
**Map** see page 81

Save this one for a day when the wind is blowing too hard to go anywhere else. If the tide is high enough to let you into the inner lagoon, you can leave the kayaks and hike over to the outer beaches and Grassy Knoll. See the previous trip for the sketchmap.

## Paddling considerations

- Crossings – insignificant
- Although not as affected by wind as most paddles, it can still be a factor.
- Can be paddled in fog by following the shoreline.

## The route

From Rosa Island, proceed south and follow the route taken by power boats. This is marked with bouys M46 and M48. Keep both to starboard. Head for the island with a dock on it, pass the floating oyster operation and follow the island's shore clockwise.

In the narrow channel behind the island, cross to the opposite shore continuing in the same direction. After a glimpse of the open ocean, continue along the same shore which eventually leads into an even narrower channel. This opens out into the inner lagoon which will be inaccessible at very low tides. In the eastern corner, there's a muddy beach and another smaller rocky one beside it. Land here and tie the boats up. A narrow trail leads to the outer shingle beaches at the mouth of Port Langford. Black bear patrol the area regularly so be prepared to give way to them. Grassy Knoll is a short hike southward.

# 17 Grassy Knoll to Rosa Island via Port Langford portage

**Difficulty** Beginner conditions – low risk
**Distance** 4 nmi one way.
**Duration** 1-2 hours
**Chart** Esperanza Inlet No. 3676, 1: 40,000, depth in metres
**Tides** on Tofino
**Currents** none

This can be a useful shortcut if the wind blows up within the shelter of the islands.

## Paddling considerations

- Inflow-outflow winds in Port Langford
- Crossings: short and protected
- In Port Langford, there are unlikely to be any boats around to assist.

## The route

Paddle round Grassy Knoll and up Port Langford to the narrow neck of land just south of the small Indian Reserve. A trail leads across to the inner lagoons. Sometimes it has been cut out but if it hasn't, veer to the north and under the trees where there is no underbrush. Scout the route first and then portage the boats. It's less than

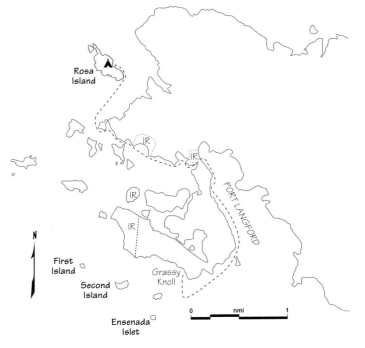

*Approaching Grassy Knoll.*

### Christian Graves

Among the people buried here are Bethine Flynn's friends, Frank and Sophie Savey. Frank, knowing he was going to die, made a tour of his friends by dugout canoe bidding them farewell. He and Sophie paddled from Nuchatlitz to Queen Cove, Flynn Cove and then to Friendly Cove. A few weeks later, he was gone.

Sophie was a laughing, happy woman who reminded Flynn of "a wren, the quick turns of her head, the eager flash in her eyes and especially, the happy chatter." She wove a traditional cedar bark cloak as a gift for Flynn. Unfortunately, she drowned at Zeballos and "came home in a box."

50 metres. The beach on the lagoon side is very muddy so try not to do this at low tide.

Once re-launched, follow the righthand shore for about 1.5 nmi. Rosa Island is visible round the next corner. The small Indian Reserve which you paddle along contains two Christian graveyards, one newer than the other. To see them, go ashore and climb a short distance up the bank and through the trees bearing west.

From the graveyards, continue on along the coast till it curves north and Rosa Island appears across a short stretch of water.

# 18 Grassy Knoll to Benson Point

**Difficulty** Advanced conditions – considerable risk
**Distance** 3 nmi one way.
**Duration** 1-1 1/2 hours
**Chart** Esperanza Inlet No. 3676, 1: 40,000, depth in metres
**Tides** on Tofino
**Currents** none

The big sandy beach round Benson Point is one of the fabulous destinations of the area. On calm days, explore the sea caves in the cliffs along the exposed shore on the way.

## Paddling considerations

- Inflow-outflow winds
- Crossing: Grassy Knoll to Belmont Point 1.1 nmi
- Surf landings. Exposure to open ocean swells. Westerly waves steepen on strong ebb tide currents creating confused seas.
- Sea fog—set compass course or stay within sight of land and put up with backwash from the cliffs.

## The route

From Grassy Knoll, head out to the Colwood Rocks and cross Port Langford to Belmont Point. It is worth a stop if you're comfortable with surf landings.

Beyond Belmont, watch for sea caves. If it's calm go into them. One has sandy beach. This stretch of coast can be subject to big swells. The Cameron Rocks and Fitz Island are home to a colony of seals but have no landings.

Watch for black bear on the beach and islands before Benson Point. It's good to know where they are foraging so that no one has any surprises. On their daily low tide patrol through their territory, they turn over rocks looking for small crabs, shore shrimp, sea worms and fish in the tide pools.

On shore, the centre of the peninsula is a garden of bluebells and rare beach carrot. The waterfall at the west end of the beach is cold and clear. Wash your hair if it's a warm day.

# 19 Benson Point to the end of Inner Basin

**Difficulty** Beginner conditions – low risk
**Distance** 5.5 nmi one way.
**Duration** 2-3 hours
**Chart** Esperanza Inlet No. 3676, 1: 40,000, depth in metres
**Tides** on Tofino
**Currents** The entrance to Inner Basin has a strong tidal current that would be hard to paddle against. Time entries and exits accordingly.

This is a welcome calm place to explore especially if you're camped at Benson Point and don't have to worry about getting back to somewhere else. Explore Laurie and Guise Creeks and let the tide carry you through into Inner Basin.

## Paddling considerations
- Some initial swells from the ocean but none inside Lord Island.
- Crossings: Benson Point to the point south of Lord Island 0.5 nmi.
- Current—see above
- Assistance could be several hours away unless there happens to be a boat anchored behind the islands.

## The route
Plan to go in to Inner Basin with the tide and return after it has turned or gone slack.

On Captain Vancouver's expedition, Peter Puget let the Chatham get too close to the entrance and got the mast tangled in the overhanging trees.

~

*A group of us shot through the entrance in fine style and then rafted up in the eddy on the other side. We read aloud an article[11] about Kendrick's purchase of land at Nuchatlitz in 1791 and just for kicks measured the latitude and longitude of his purchase. It proved to be in the open ocean. This was because his naviga-*

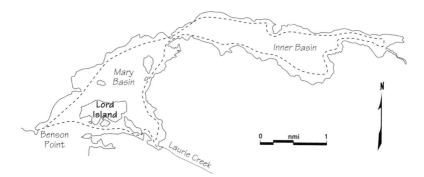

*Mary Basin looking toward the entrance to Inner Basin.*

*tional measuring instruments were inaccurate. Cook had one of the first really accurate chronometers so his longitude measurements are correct even today.*

~

Inner Basin is not particularly interesting. There are a couple of pretty islands half way down but it's difficult to land anywhere.

Back in Mary Basin itself, Guise Creek is a shady walk on a hot day but rough underfoot. It is the best place to refill water containers.

At high tide, you can paddle right up to the Laurie Creek waterfall but at low tide, very slimy rocks make it lethal to approach. Also at low tide, the big expanse of shingle is alive with bears in search of crustaceans and other goodies. They like the taste of the plastic water pipe which supplies a cabin in the next bay and chew on it.

Inside the protection of Lord Island, the water is very calm and yachts often come in to anchor.

# 20 Nuchatlitz to Tongue Point

**Difficulty** Advanced conditions – considerable risk.
**Distance** 3-4 nmi one way.
**Duration** 1-1 1/2 hours
**Chart** Esperanza Inlet No. 3676, 1: 40,000, depth in metres
**Tides** on Tofino
**Currents** none

Under calm weather conditions, this trip is a fabulous open ocean crossing, passing outer rocks and skerries with opportunities to view unique bird and sea life. There's lots to see and do around Tongue Point so it's worth moving camp over there for a few days.

## Paddling considerations

- Must only be done on a clear calm day when the forecast is for continued good weather.

- If the weather changes part-way across, divert to Mary Basin or return to camp.
- Sea fog
- Crossings. The whole trip is a crossing — 3-4 nmi depending on where you launch.
- There is no place to land safely on the outer skerries. Pee before leaving!
- Take extra meals and possibly overnight camping gear.
- Set a compass course before leaving. Watch for incoming fog or the south wind which brings it.
- Carry 200 feet of line to tie the kayaks in Louie Bay when the tide is low.

## The route

Once clear of the Nuchatlitz Islands, paddle along the compass course or just head for the inside of Ferrer Point. En route, watch for rafts of sea otters and stop to watch them. Flocks of black oystercatchers often tintinnabulate around the skerries, their red beaks gleaming in the sunshine. At low tide, examine the outer edges of the skerries carefully. Sea palm seaweed only grows in places where there is a constant surge. It looks like small palm trees. Be careful that your boat doesn't get washed onto a rocky ledge by a swell.

## Fatality

On May 19, 2003 the *MV Lady Frances Barkley* dropped two kayakers at Esperanza. (She was filling in for the *MV Uchuck* away on her annual refit.) The crew, who were used to transporting kayakers in Barkley Sound, thought the two men in their mid thirties were better equipped than many kayakers they had seen. The kayakers did not book a return trip and the crew thought they would likely paddle down Tahsis Inlet to be picked up again at one of the *Uchuck's* regular stops like Plumper Harbour or Mooyah Bay. This didn't happen.

Gale-force winds on Saturday May 24 forced a power boat to run for shelter from 5-6 metre swells pounding into Nuchatlitz Inlet. As it passed rocky Ensenada Island the crew noticed a human body washed up on the rocks and called the Coast Guard.

The Coast Guard vessel Gordon Reed conducted a water search. The RCMP were also involved. A Cormorant helicopter flew a Canadian Ranger Group from Gold River and the Campbell River Search and Rescue to Louie Bay to conduct a land search. Sgt. Scott Parker of the Rangers said the weather on the Monday was "snarly with a big surf running and two-metre swells."

The chopper found a second body on Third Beach and the land party discovered a bashed up kayak on the rocks 300 metres north toward Ferrer Point. Bits of the second kayak were found later.

*Esenada from Third Island.*

As you approach the other side, head east along the shore from Ferrer Point until Louie Bay opens up. Keep an eye out for whale spouts. Often there's a grey whale or two about.

~

*One sunny morning as three of us approached Tongue Point, the other two went ahead and disappeared around the corner. I was within 100 metres of the beach when I noticed a small triangular rock I didn't remember seeing on the chart. I checked again and there was no mention of it.*

*When I looked up I couldn't see it. The water had a bit of a ripple which I concluded was obscuring it. Then I glanced back toward Nuchatlitz. Now there was a long low grey reef where there had been none before. The reef snuffled a bit. I remembered a photograph I had seen taken in the Baja of a grey whale swimming under a kayak just before it flipped the boat. I had met orca in Johnstone Strait and had stopped paddling while they swam past. Would this creature leave me alone or become aggressive like the one in the photo? With trembling hands, I opened my spray skirt and got my camera out. If something happened to me, I wanted to leave a record of the cause. I clicked one picture, then another. As I clicked the second, the grey whale's tail came up out of the water showing a perfect vee as the animal sounded. Happily, I paddled to catch up with the others.*

~

On reaching Tongue Point, round it and go into Louie Bay which dries completely at low tide. Tie the boats together and to a long line fastened to a tree root. Don't leave them untied and unattended as the tide comes in very quickly and even if you are on shore, it's a continual relay race to pull them up before the tide gets them.

The large unsightly pieces of metal on the shore are all that remains of a 16,000 ton Greek freighter, *Treis Ierarchi*, which ran aground on the rocks off Ferrer Point on December 7, 1969. All 28 crew were rescued. Later, when the price of scrap metal was high, salvagers towed the wreck into Louie Bay where they blew it up into smaller pieces. Scrap metal prices promptly dropped so they abandoned their prize and there it lies.

There's a small level grassy meadow just inside Tongue Point. Bushwhack to find the trail up the hill to disused Camp Ferrier. It's about a 10 minute walk. Watch for bear in the meadow. Mink run in and out of the deserted decaying buildings some of which are not safe to enter. A trail from the dining room goes farther up the hill to where they used to turn on the water supply. The remains of a boardwalk are slippery with algae.

At low tide, walk out to the islands in Louie Bay watching for deer prints in the sand. Flocks of shore birds wheel around. If the tide is high, kayak across the bay to where the chart shows a "passage" through to the ocean. Likely it exists on a high storm tide but normally there's a small inlet which narrows past a deserted trailer and becomes too shallow to paddle. It's a short scramble to where you can see the ocean battering the rocks on the outer coast. In the evening, listen for a call wilder than a loon's—wolf howls.

# 21 Tongue Point to Third Beach via the lagoon

**Difficulty** Beginner conditions – low risk
**Distance** 2.5 nmi one way
**Duration** 2-3 hours
**Chart** Esperanza Inlet No. 3676, 1: 40,000, depth in metres
**Tides** on Tofino
**Currents** Tidal current in and out of the lagoon.

An all-day trip to a magical outer beach.

## Paddling considerations

- Entry into the lagoon depends on tide level. Mid tide is best.
- No boats around to assist.

## The route

On the way in to Louie Bay, check the entrance to the lagoon east of it and predict what it's going to be like in the morning. Take boots, and pack a backpack with lunch, bathing suit, sunscreen and mosquito repellant.

Once through the entrance, keep left. Sooner rather than later, you'll run out of water and have to tow and haul the kayak through shallow channels about half way down the lagoon. Going to the right sometimes looks better but it isn't. The paddle down the rest of the lake is short. Float planes may land bringing Nootka Trail hikers. At the head of the lagoon, tie the boats and begin hiking.

The half-hour hike takes this long because the trail goes over and under huge slippery old growth logs, through salal jungle and across mud wallows and creeks. Watch for wolf footprints in the mud. If they're filling with water, the perpetrators are likely watching you. Wolves have attacked dogs here so don't bring them.

The locals, who probably counted the beaches around Camp Ferrier, have always called this beach "Third Beach" but a recent guide to the Nootka Trail, which starts here, mistakenly calls it "First Beach."

Once Nootka Trail hikers come out on the beach, they will head to the left where a rope assists them to climb up over the first point. Large Pacific rollers crash down on the steeply sloping beach which has a strong undertow. Watch for cougar prints in the sand. At the far right beyond the rocky outcrops, the surf is much gentler. After casing the situation, adventurous paddlers may decide to paddle around Ferrer Point and do a surf landing (see Trip 22).

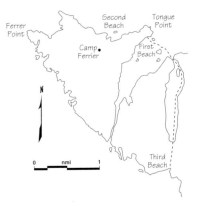

# 22 Rosa Island to Friendly Cove on the outside

**Difficulty** Advanced conditions – considerable risk
**Distance** 26 nmi one way.
**Duration** 10-12 hour
**Chart** Nootka Sound to Quatsino Sound No. LC 3604, 1:150,000, depth in metres
**Tides** on Tofino
**Currents** none

An open ocean paddle to some truly fabulous beaches.

## Paddling considerations

- Proficiency in surf landings essential

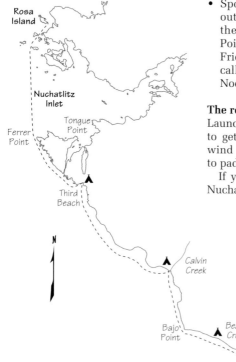

- Inflow-outflow winds in Nuchatlitz Inlet
- Fog wind
- Crossings: Nuchatlitz Inlet 4 nmi
- Boomers and clapotis off Bajo Point
- Sport fishing boats speeding without looking. In Nuchatlitz Inlet, they'll be heading from Ferrer Point back to Esperanza. Around Friendly Cove—the Zoo as they call it – they'll be heading back into Nootka Sound.

## The route

Launch early between 5 am and 6 am to get as far as possible before the wind comes up. It's a gorgeous time to paddle.

If you want a break after crossing Nuchatlitz Inlet (see Trip 20), come in

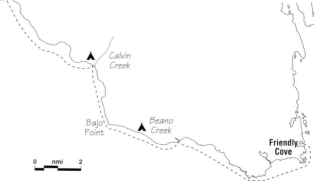

*Bumper surf at Third beach.*

at the north end of Third Beach to land. There's camping space if required.

Most paddlers then head for Calvin Creek which is 5 nmi farther south. Now that the Nootka Trail has become popular, you may see parties of hikers on the beach from time to time. After a work party from the Comox Valley Hikers cleared the trail, the Mowachaht/Muchalaht Band announced they are charging hikers $40 each to use it.

Calvin Creek is a surf landing. A waterfall spills down into a deep pool on the sandy beach before the creek runs out into the ocean. The water, which comes from Crawfish Lake, is cold. Great if you build a tarp sauna on the beach.

~

*Scottish paddler, Eric Watterson, went for "a wee paddle" from Nuchatlitz one day. (This man has been paddling the Hebrides for the last thirty years. He's also done West Greenland, the Baltic and most of the British Isles. He builds his own boats including the take-apart he brought with him.) He crossed to Tongue Point where he saw two grey whales then continued round Ferrer Point and down the coast to Calvin Creek where he landed.*

*As he pulled his boat up, he saw a wolf cub come out of the forest above the beach and then another. He whistled at the cubs and one howled. He howled back but the two had had enough and melted back into the trees. Never having seen wild wolves before, he paddled back to camp in a state of ecstacy.*

~

The next landmark is Bajo Point 3 nmi south of Calvin Creek. This is a hazardous area with boomers and offshore kelp beds.

~

*Experienced SKABC paddlers, Tony, Dana and Jacquie, were paddling in echelon formation heading south with swells about 1½ metres high. They got through the first section and Tony had just said to Dana, "It looks like we made it," when he saw a huge wave coming. He paddled toward it and went up and over. Dana did the same. Tony turned and saw Jacquie on top of the wave which was breaking under her. Luckily she knew how to handle surf and the rock underneath was deep enough that she didn't touch it.*

~

Beano Creek is 3 nmi farther on. Be prepared for a surf landing here too, though the beach has a protective bar which at some tide levels you may be able to get behind. The creek is warmer for swimming than Calvin and the pea gravel beach makes for good camping. As there's now a hiker's B&B here and logging road access over the island to Plumper Harbour, it's not complete wilderness.

From Beano Creek to Maquinna Point and the lagoon beyond, there are few landing places, mostly very rocky. The lagoon is accessible at high tide but is surrounded by privately owned cabins. In this area, watch for fast moving sport fishing boats. If they're catching fish, they may not be paying much attention to anything else on the water.

Beyond the lagoon, the long grey shingle beach at Friendly Cove curves round. A surf landing half way along it, brings you close to the camping area. You pay the Band member at the church. If you land without camping, there is a landing fee.

## Camp Ferrier

From 1948-1992, the Esperanza Mission operated a popular summer youth program called Ferrier Point Bible Camp. Louise Johnson, who wrote a history of the Mission, says that over the years this mispronunciation of Ferrer Point became accepted.

They chose the place because a building left over from a World War II radar station was available for the cafeteria and they built other sleeping cabins around the meadow. Ships such as the *Messenger III* , the *Donna Dene*, which sank one night at the entrance to Louie Bay when no one was aboard, and the *Uchuck III* brought the children from their homes as far away as Kyuquot and Port Alberni and transported supplies from Esperanza.

For ten days in July the children ran wild. They hiked, swam, played volleyball and badminton and sang round beach fires in the evening. To this day many stories are told about the rough seas on the voyage to and from the camp. Young Dorothea McLean listened to the breakers and shivered in bed dreading the next day's journey. Aboard ship, she always stood next to her father, Dr. McLean.

"Are we going to sink, Dad?" she'd ask.

"Yes dear. Of course we're going to sink," was always his answer.

# 23 Nuchatlitz to Catala Island Spit

**Difficulty** Advanced conditions – considerable risk
**Distance** 3 nmi one way.
**Duration** 1 hour
**Chart** Esperanza Inlet No. 3676, 1: 40,000, depth in metres
**Tides** on Tofino
**Currents** none

An open ocean crossing which needs to be timed for good weather. Look for pelagic birds like murres, pigeon guillemots, rhinocerous auklets and pairs of marbled murrelets.

## Paddling considerations

- Bad weather blows up very quickly. Same day return might not be possible. Take overnight gear plus food and water.
- Set compass course in case of fog
- Crossing: Rosa Island to the East end of Catala 2 nmi

## The route

Open ocean swells roll in on the outside of the Nuchatlitz Islands. Check that everyone is comfortable with this before proceeding farther. You can always just circumnavigate Rosa Island instead.

Out in the swells, paddle steadily aiming either for Black Rock off the easterly point of Catala or for Twin Islands. Many people, intrigued by the small grove of trees, like to land there. It's apt to be windy, so most don't stay long but continue on to circumnavigate Catala in a clockwise direction.

If the wind has come up, head for Black Rock, the island's easterly point and the shelter behind them. At high tide, the sea caves between here and the triangular spit where the campsite is are well worth exploring.

At the spit, be prepared for a surf landing and use a long line to hang onto the boats or the undertow will suck them out immediately.

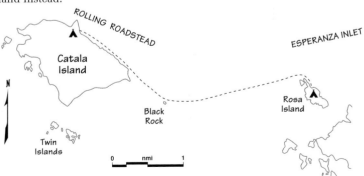

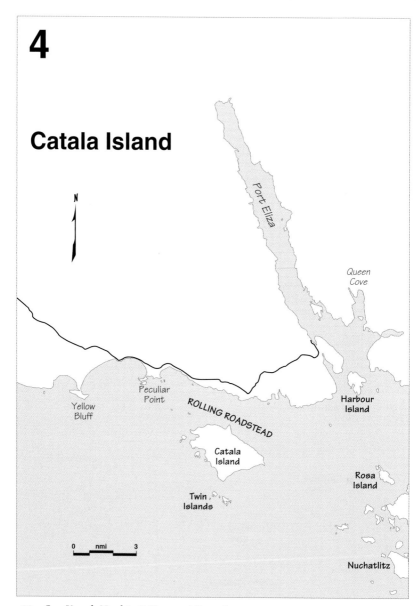

**4**

# Catala Island

N

Port Eliza

Queen
Cove

Yellow
Bluff

Peculiar
Point

ROLLING ROADSTEAD

Harbour
Island

Catala
Island

0    nmi    3

Twin
Islands

Rosa
Island

Nuchatlitz

Sea caves are one of the main attractions of Catala Island. The ones between the camp spot and the Indian Reserve are best explored at high tide. There is also a large sea cave at the west end of the island.

A trail leads to the lake and bog in the centre of the island. Trees exposed to on-shore winds from the ocean are twisted and bent. When exploring, stay away from the Indian Reserve at the east end. It is not in the park.

In calm weather, commercial fishing boats and others sometimes anchor overnight in Rolling Roadstead but when rough weather produces swells, they will head for the shelter of Queen Cove and Port Eliza.

Catala Island Marine Provincial Park is a popular camping spot with lots of room and shelter from on-shore winds. However, head to the mainland if there is a tsunami warning.

Catala is a convenient centre from which to do trips to Yellow Bluff, Queen Cove, Port Eliza and Nuchatlitz. It can accommodate several large groups of campers.

## Launches

The *MV Uchuck* passes on the inside of Catala Island on Thursdays, returning on Fridays. See Esperanza Inlet.

## Camping Locations:

### Catala Island

The triangular spit on the north side has room for lots of groups of campers, but water has to be obtained from one of the creeks on the mainland opposite. Although the island shelters the camp area from the winds, the steep shingle beach has a surge on it which can make landing difficult. Use slings and four people to carry loaded boats up the bank—or use a long line to tie them to driftwood at the top. This campsite has one pit toilet. If making fire, use an existing fire ring and never make fire against a log.

Camping on the west side is less crowded, very windy and may require surf landings. Do not camp on the Indian Reserve.

### Father Megin Catala

Father Megín Catalá (1761-1830) was one of the Franciscan chaplains to the Spanish garrison at Santa Cruz de Nuca, which is what the Spanish called Friendly Cove. He is depicted in the stained glass window in the church at Friendly Cove talking to the Indians. Little is known about him except that he was unable to return in 1794.

The chaplains' main duties were to look after the Europeans. These were seamen from the Naval Department of San Blas, near Puerta Vallarta, Mexico, and the soldiers belonging to the Second Company of the Catalonian Volunteers.

It was quite common for young native people to be invited south to learn Spanish ways. In 1791, one such 19 -year-old woman was baptized Maria de Jesus de Nuca. She lived a life of comparative luxury as a ward of the Governor. Her descendent, Geraldine Shelley from San Diego, discovered that Elder Sam Johnson of the A'haminaquus Reserve remembered that "the sister of one of my grandmothers" had left on such a voyage.

## High Rocks

On October 2nd 1948, Dr. Herman McLean of Esperanza and his 15-year-old son Bruce were returning from Chamiss Bay in Kyuquot Sound. The water was so rough that it was five hours before they got inside Tatchu Point. Their engine stopped and Dr. McLean went below to find that the gasline and bilge were full of water. He tried to pump it out but the pump broke. With no radio, they were unable to call for help.

"Let's stick together, Dad," said Bruce as the boat foundered on a rock. They were the last words he uttered before the waves swept him to his death. Dr. McLean swam and swam till his lungs almost burst. After hitting the bottom of the boat, he burst into the air and grabbed a dark object. It was Bruce who was already dead. He let go as the waves hurled him against a rock, then pulled him off to slap him against another one. He hung on and climbed to the top of High Rocks where the waves splattered him every five minutes. In the morning, he saw that the ship was sitting on a nearby shelf. He salvaged some rope, wet blankets and a few cans of food. When the tide came up again, he lashed himself to the rock and prayed. Forty-eight hours after the sinking, a fishboat rescued him.

# 24 Circumnavigation of Catala Island

**Difficulty** Intermediate conditions – moderate risk
**Distance** 4 nmi.
**Duration** 2-3 hours
**Chart** Esperanza Inlet No. 3676, 1: 40,000, depth in metres
**Tides** on Tofino
**Currents** none

Sea caves and a visit to the Twin Islands are the main attractions.

## Paddling considerations

- Inflow-outflow winds, in Esperanza Inlet especially
- Rock garden at the west end—dangerous in fog. Turn back and try another day.
- Crossing: Catala to Twin Islands 0.5 nmi

## The route

Can be done in either direction. The decision will depend on the weather. The northwest end of the island is guarded by a rock garden which compounds swells from the open ocean into confused water. Somewhere in this area, there is a large cave that can be paddled into. Inside, the water is calm. I have never found it, but I have spoken to people who are vehement that it exists.

Twin Islands off the south shore are a possible haunt for nesting black oystercatchers. Step carefully and leave if the birds seem in distress as their usually single egg is almost indistinguishable from the shingle.

On the northeast side of the island, numerous sea caves are best explored at high tide.

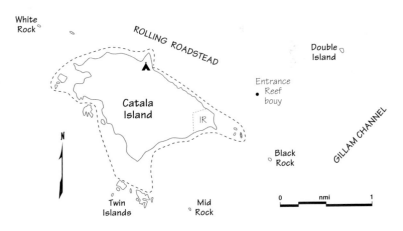

# 25 Catala Island to Queen Cove

**Difficulty** Intermediate conditions – moderate risk
**Distance** 4 nmi one way.
**Duration** 1 1/2 hours
**Chart** Esperanza Inlet No. 3676, 1: 40,000, depth in metres
**Tides** on Tofino
**Currents** none

Queen Cove is a small Indian village overlooked by the last surviving church built by Father Brabant. Behind the village there's a big sheltered cove where yachts anchor.

### Paddling considerations
- Inflow-outflow winds
- Crossings
  - Rolling Roadstead 0.4 nmi
  - Harbour Island to Queen Cove 0.7 nmi
- Sea fog—set a compass course before leaving.

### The route
Cross Rolling Roadstead and follow the shore in an easterly direction. Pink cliffs guard the entrance to Port Eliza. On the inside of Harbour Island, cross diagonally to the village.

Land beside the dock and ask permission to visit the church. An overgrown trail goes up the hill to it. Watch for rotted timbers with nails in them and broken glass. The windows are long gone and so are the big church bell and the dugout canoe which were once kept inside. The floor may no longer be safe.

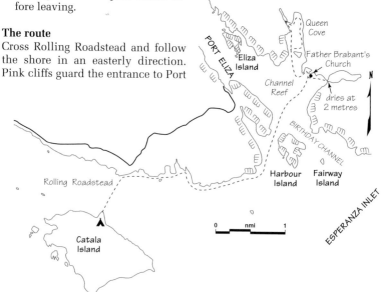

*Approaching Queen Cove.*

### Father Brabant

Father Augustin Brabant (1845-1912) came to the West Coast from Belgium in 1869 and founded his first mission at Hesquiat in 1875. He regularly travelled from Barkley Sound to the Brooks Peninsula hitching rides on trading schooners, gun boats and in dugout canoes. In bad weather, Queen Cove was a popular sheltered anchorage for these ships.

The good Father built his own churches, first at Hesquiat in 1874 and then others farther north at Kyuquot, Queen Cove, Nuchatlitz and Friendly Cove. When neither sealing schooners nor gun boats were available, he travelled by canoe with his parishioners visiting Nuu-chah-nulth people from Barkley Sound to the Brooks Peninsula.

On the Esperanza Inlet side of Queen Cove, there is a small tidal lagoon. Before entering, land and scout the tidal rapids. Unless the tide is high, the rocks in the centre may hole the bottom of an unsuspecting paddler's kayak. Very inconvenient—especially if you're not carrying a fibreglass repair kit or plenty of duct tape.

Behind the village of Queen Cove, a large sheltered lagoon often contains pleasure boats circumnavigating Vancouver Island. There are also some cottages.

# 26 Queen Cove to the Head of Port Eliza

**Difficulty** Intermediate conditions – moderate risk
**Distance** 5 nmi one way.
**Duration** 2 hours
**Chart** Esperanza Inlet No. 3676, 1: 40,000, depth in metres
**Tides** on Tofino
**Currents** none

Although there's nothing particular to
see at the head of Port Eliza except a
fish farm or two, this trip might produce a welcome sunny respite if sea
fog blankets the outer coast.

### Paddling considerations
- Inflow-outflow winds
- Crossings: none
- Few places to land
- Availability of rescue boats uncer-
  tain

### The route
Leaving Queen Cove, turn west and
paddle past Eliza Island. There's a
small fairly sheltered rocky cove
on the outside of it. In August, the
huckleberry bushes are laden with red
fruit. Beyond the island, the inlet has
many cliffs and a few landing places.
Boats sometimes seek shelter and
anchorage behind a narrow peninsula
less than a mile from the head. There
may be fish farms part way up and at
the head of the inlet. Go up one side
and down the other.

On the way back just past Eliza
Island, but on the west shore, there's
a cove containing a log dump and a
dock. The *Uchuck* regularly calls in
with supplies for the logging camp
several miles down the road near
Peculiar Point. Sometimes a Fisheries
inspection boat moors here.

# 27 Catala Island to Yellow Bluff

**Difficulty** Intermediate conditions – moderate risk
**Distance** 3 nmi one way.
**Duration** 2-3 hours
**Chart** Esperanza Inlet No. 3676, 1: 40,000, depth in metres
**Tides** on Tofino
**Currents** none

Isolated sandy beaches and a lovely waterfall are the prizes bestowed by this paddle.

## Paddling considerations

- Inflow-outflow winds
- Crossings
  - Northwest end of Catala to Yellow Bluff 2 nmi
  - Rolling Roadstead 0.4 nmi.
- Surf landings.
- Sea fog a possibility

## The route

Weather permitting, cross direct from the north end of Catala to Yellow Bluff. Digress to High Rocks. Even in bright sun, they are a bit spooky.

Proceed on to a surf landing at Yellow Bluff. The extreme western end of the beach may have less surf. It's a lovely sandy beach with a fringe of trees in front of a clearcut. A logging road follows the shore between Port Eliza and Kapoose Creek to the north.

On the way back, watch for a waterfall and land for a cold fresh-water shower. Lovely on a hot day. Sometimes a grey whale takes up residence in the cove before Peculiar Point. It will spend all day alternately feeding on the bottom and coming up to breathe. With it's big baleen jaw, it ploughs a massive bite out of the sand and filters out the krill on which it feeds.

Follow the shoreline back, crossing over at the narrow point of Rolling Roadstead where the Catala camping area juts out. There's a big cave at the west end of the shingle bar which you may already have explored on a campground stroll.

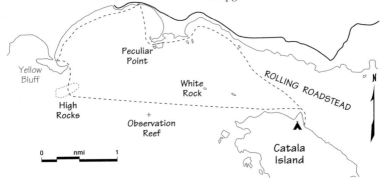

# 28 Yellow Bluff to Rugged Point

**Difficulty** Advanced conditions – considerable risk
**Distance** 12 nmi one way.
**Duration** 6-8 hours
**Charts** Kyuquot Sound No.3682, 1:36,676, depth in fathoms and Nootka Sound to Quatsino Sound No. LC 3604, 1:150,000, depth in metres
**Tides** on Tofino
**Currents** none

## Paddling considerations
- Exposed ocean
- Surf landings
- Extensive reefs off Tatchu Point requiring an offshore detour of 1-2 nmi.
- Sea fog—Wait till it lifts or risk being blown out to sea.

## The route
Be on the water at first light when the sea is calmest. Listen carefully to the weather forecasts both for north and south Vancouver Island as Tatchu Point is the boundary between the two.

An open ocean trip requiring an offshore detour to get round Tatchu Point. The rewards are access to tiny island groups rarely frequented by paddlers, puffin colonies, extensive deserted sandy beaches suitable for camping. A trip for advanced paddlers only.

To round Tatchu Point, you have to paddle a mile or two offshore to avoid the treacherous boomers that guard the point. Chart No. LC3604 Nootka Sound to Quatsino shows the problem more clearly than the Kyuquot Sound chart. Keep on the outside of the 30 metre depth contour.

Once round Tatchu, land at Jurassic Point if need be. Check the rocks for fossil ammonite and belemnites.

Proceed up Clear Passage or explore the islands which shelter it. On the edge of bull kelp beds look for puffins and rhinoceros auklets. There is a tufted puffin colony on Clark Island next to Grassy Island. Examine it through binoculars, but don't get close enough that the birds fly off the nesting ledges. Gulls steal the eggs while they're away and a whole generation is lost.

To land on Grassy Island approach it from the northeast. Rocks form a bay round a gravel beach. Once ashore, hunt for fossils and rare plants as Grassy, like the Brooks Peninsula, escaped the ice age. Look and photograph but leave them in place for the next person to enjoy.

Rugged Point Provincial Park, which is still in the territory of the Ehattesaht Nation, starts at Kapoose Creek. The outer coast beaches are superb. Consider camping here instead of at Rugged Point which is likely to be crowded. Just south of Gross Point, sheltering reefs make the landing easier. Hikers have likely come from Rugged Point or been dropped off for the day by water taxis.

The main Rugged Point campsite is on the north side of Rugged Point. There are two tent pads and limited tenting space adjacent to them. Near-

## Sea Otters

Sea otters became extinct on the B.C. coast in the early 1800s due to over hunting. They were re-introduced to the Bunsby Islands north of Kyuquot in the sixties and have now spread south to Bajo Point on Nootka Island.

Sea otters *Enhydra lutris* are a much larger and different species from the land otters *Lontra canadensis* with which most people are familiar. They live most of their lives in the kelp beds. Their fur is denser than that of any other animal. The outer guard hairs form a continuous waterproof cover for the soft underfur which remains dry and keeps the animal warm. Constant grooming is essential to keep the outer fur from matting in clumps which would defeat the system. Their loosely fitting coat can easily be pulled on to their bellies for grooming which is what the otters are often doing when seen floating on their backs. They seldom come ashore.

Unfortunately, they compete with First Nations' people for sea urchins. This conflict has been documented in Canadian Geographic video: The Dance of the Sea Otter 47 minutes.

by, a roofed picnic shelter contains a large table and benches with four metal bear-proof food caches up a short trail.

A winding boardwalk through a grove of old growth Douglas fir forest leads past a pit toilet to the beaches on the south side of the peninsula. Bear and cougar are regular visitors to the area.

*Yellow Bluff with Eliza Dome repeater station above.*

### Sometimes it's Wise to Turn Back

I planned a small side trip on my own to go round Tatchu Point. After a night camped at the end of Yellow Bluff, a beautiful sandy crescent beach, I was on the water in the dark calm before sunrise, fully equipped with wetsuit on and all safety equipment to hand. Within 30 minutes the wind began to blow the tops off the waves so at High Rocks I turned back to spend a day beachcombing and playing under the waterfall near Peculiar Point before returning to the others on Catala. Bud, who had rounded Tatchu once before and required three days rest to recover from his white-knuckle journey said: "I told you so!"

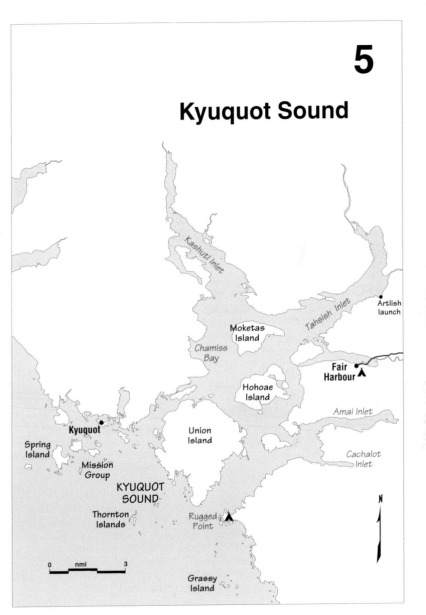

**5**

**Kyuquot Sound**

Kashutl Inlet

Tahsish Inlet

Artlish launch

Moketas Island

Chamiss Bay

Fair Harbour

Hohoae Island

Amai Inlet

Kyuquot

Union Island

Cachalot Inlet

Spring Island

Mission Group

KYUQUOT SOUND

Thornton Islands

Rugged Point

N

0    nmi    3

Grassy Island

*Air Nootka scheduled flight loading at Kyuquot.*

The Bunsby Islands and the Rugged Point beaches are the main attractions that bring sea kayakers to Kyuquot Sound. Although the Bunsby's are included in this section, the launches are the same as for Kyuquot.

Kyuquot Sound is the traditional territory of the Kyuquot people. As it was geographically remote from the Department of Indian Affairs, First Nations people have retained much more of their self confidence and dignity than those elsewhere. Today, they both demand respect and receive it. The Coast Guard rely on their expertise for search and rescue.

Apart from a few fish farms and logging camps, most people live in the settlement of Kyuquot at the mouth of the sound. It has no road access so those who don't fly in on the scheduled Air Nootka service from Gold River, have to go by boat from road ends at either Fair Harbour or Artlish.

The inlets are subject to strong winds, so travel very early or late. Landing and camping places are scarce so it's best to travel in daylight. In the early twentieth century, there were mines, traplines, salteries and even a whaling station in these inlets. Their remains can be explored when fog blankets the coast and paddlers long for sunshine again. That's the time to explore the inlets.

Like Venice, Kyuquot is built on several islands. It has navigational aides instead of traffic lights. Although it has a state of the art telephone system, most people communicate on VHF Channel 14. That's how you call the motel or the water taxi service in this area.

When paddling in to Kyuquot, watch for float planes coming out at speed. As there isn't much space for kayaks to land by the government dock on Walter's Island, paddle farther west and walk back along the trail which runs the length of the island.

In years gone by, the Europeans lived on Walter's Island while the original inhabitants lived on the Houpcitas Reserve across the water. These divisions are slowly becoming blurred. The hospital, a nursing station, and other houses are scattered around neighbouring islands.

Walter, who the island is named after, was a storekeeper whose house burnt down in the 1970s. As only one boat fishes out of Kyuquot, the fish plant is largely idle. The government and seaplane docks are busier. The combined general store and post office is located beside the dock. It is operated by the Kayra family whose parents arrived to fish in the 1920s.

Miss Charlie's Restaurant is seldom open so don't rely on it—importing food for the odd passerby is just too expensive. However, there are one or two bed and breakfast places which will be full on Thursday nights when the *MV Uchuck* passengers stay overnight.

Located across the water are the motel, the kayak shop and water taxi, the Band Office, the school and more houses. Walk up the street which runs down to the dock. On the right a block back from it, a sign identifies the Band Office. The Kyuquot Nation would like visitors to make a courtesy call here especially if they have not replied to your letter asking permission to camp. They maintain a sign

*Seaplane taking off from Kyuquot.*

in book where you may leave details of contact numbers to be used in case of emergency. Pick up the latest brochures and consider purchasing waterproof maps of the area. They also have a new native-designed sea otter T-shirt. Ask if there's a red tide making the shellfish inedible and ask about the dates and locations of their Rediscovery Camp for native young people. This is often held at Rugged Point, Spring Island or Battle Bay. Organiser Alex Jules says kayakers are welcome to drop in at any time to visit.

Near the dock, Leo Jack operates a kayak store in conjunction with his Voyager Water Taxi service. Phone ahead for a reservation. The store sells ice cream, local handicrafts and kayaking gear.

While you're there, pay a visit to Elders Sarah and Alex Short, who in exchange for a donation, will tell you stories about the history of Kyuquot. See the work they do with cedar-bark grass and meet local carvers. As there is 80% unemployment in Kyuquot, the donation is important. Buy locally whenever possible. The communities on both sides of the water, need your business.

### Launches

Fair Harbour and Artlish are the only road access points to this area. (Other logging roads visible from the water in remote areas such as behind Kyuquot do not link up with those connected to the main highway system.)

Launching at Fair Harbour or Artlish, paddlers can access Rugged Point, Kyuquot and the South Brooks

### Kyuquot's Last Great War

When Kyuquot people talk of "the last war," they do not mean World War II. They mean the war when several other Nuu-chah-nulth tribes from the south sent a force of 400 warriors to attack the Kyuquot summer village on Aktis Island. At midnight on a moonless night in 1855, 400 warriors of various tribes organized by the Clayoquots from the Tofino area attacked the sleeping village. A minute before they landed, two Kyuquots returning home late yelled "Weena! Weena!" (Strangers! Danger!) The sleepers, who had been expecting the attack for so long that they had relaxed their guard, grabbed their weapons. In the confusion, one man shot his own daughter. Crazed by grief he then shot three Clayoquots before being killed himself. Part of the village went up in flames. Survivors fled to the chief's house barricading themselves in as muskets crackled all around. Kyuquot stories tell of two or three enemy being felled with a single shot, they were so close together. When expected reinforcements failed to show, the disgruntled invaders retreated, blaming each other, although they had 35 heads and 13 slaves to show for their attack. Kyuquot people still talk of this event.

Peninsula or they can explore the two upper inlets of Kyuquot Sound—a good choice if sea fog is blanketing the outer coast.

VHF, including weather radio reception in Fair Harbour and almost to the mouth of Kyuquot Sound, is not available. Check satellite images on the internet before leaving home for current weather forecasts and some idea of upcoming weather systems. Once out of the inlets, most local people monitor VHF Channel 14.

Some people hire Kyuquot boatmen to transport their kayaks from Fair Harbour or Artlish to a destination such as Rugged Point, the Bunsby Islands or the South Brooks. Kyuquot has an excellent telephone system so make these arrangements before leaving home. Costs are in the $300-$500 range per boat load. Instead of a two day paddle, the water taxi can get you to the Bunsby Islands in about an hour and a half. (For contacts, see page 163)

## Fair Harbour

From Campbell River, drive north on Highway 19 to Woss. Continue on Highway 19 until the sign for Zeballos Forest Service Road. This is the end of the pavement and the beginning of an active logging road used at all hours by heavy equipment. Zeballos is 42 km and Fair Harbour is 74 km. The road is in good condition but drive with caution obeying the 60 km speed limit. There are a number of well sign-posted forks in the road. For about an hour, follow the signs for Zeballos. It's a pretty little gold mining town with an interesting museum and a general store. Phone to get someone to open the gas pump if the store is closed.

On the outskirts of Zeballos, a road to Fair Harbour will by-pass the town. Initially, the road skirts the relocated Ehatishat Indian Reserve and speed bumps force vehicles to slow down. This is the correct road. Shortly after, pass the entrance to Resolution Park. Do not be tempted to drive down to its inviting beach without having four-wheel drive to get back out again. Drive for about an hour past Little Espinosa Inlet, pass the turn off to Oclucje, the relocated Nuchatlitz Indian Reserve, and continue on to where the Kaouk River debouches into a wide estuary. The road crosses a bridge and Fair Harbour appears.

In the 1950s, Fair Harbour was a bustling Western Forest Products logging camp which closed in the 1970s. For a while only summer fishermen and their families lived there in trailers and tents. Recently, Swan Enterprises have bought property adjacent to the dock and are operating a propane tank refilling station along with a small store selling chocolate bars, T-shirts and fishing lures. They now charge for camping beside the best kayak launch spots—a great convenience. They will also look after vehicles for a daily fee. In addition to money, they want the name and phone number of a contact person who they will drive into Zeballos to phone if paddlers do not return on the due date specified. That person would then be responsible for contacting the Coast Guard to initiate a search in conjunction with Kyuquot Band members who know every nook and

*Lunch stop at Guillod Point.*

crannie in the area. This is a service well worth paying for. Before its advent, vandalism was common.

## Artlish

The Artlish launch is 0.7 nmi south of where the Artlish River enters Tahsish Inlet three miles north of the entrance to Fair Harbour. It cuts an hour off the road journey but there is no camping at the launch and no one looks after vehicles. Camp at Atluk Lake and drive down in the morning. This put-in is mainly used by Kyuquot residents. I was advised that the road has some dangerous curves, especially if you meet a logging truck on them, and steep hills which can be a problem with two-wheel drive vehicles, though some have made it.

## Camping Locations

To preserve culturally sensitive areas, before camping in their territory, the Kyuquot people ask that you obtain permission from the Band Office in Kyuquot. On the matter of camping, Leo Jack who runs the Voyager water taxi has authority to speak for his aunt, Christina Cox, the Kyuquot Chief. In addition there are the following campsites.

### Fair Harbour

1. A small privately operated campground near the launch. Ask at the store which also operates a supervised long-term parking area.

2. Away from the launch, a BC Forest Service campground of 25 units largely taken up by summer sport fishers and their RVs.

## Rugged Point
### BC Parks campground
The main camping area is where the provincial park sign is located just past Robin Point. There are a couple of tent pads and a roomy picnic shelter with a large table and benches. Behind it, food can be cached in four metal cupboards up a short trail. A boardwalk leads across the headland, past a pit toilet, to a sandy beach on the south coast. There is no water. Many more campers arrive than the tent pads can accommodate. Some scrounge places along the beach.

### Rugged Point – outside beaches
These beaches require surf landings. If you have the skill, you'll get a fabulous campsite. For water, hike or paddle to Kapoose Creek or take Trip 36 to Union Island.

### Spring Island
Unorganized beach camping connected by a 600-metre trail across the island. No potable water is available. An old brochure suggests digging cat-holes in the intertidal zone for human wastes where strong water action exists. It does not exist here. Please use the pit toilet at the entrance to the trail.

The west side of the inner bay is permanently taken up by West Coast Expeditions, a well-respected eco-tourist company which has operated here in cooperation with the Kyuquot Nation for several decades.

The east side of the bay has a number of sites back in the bush.

A bay on the south side of the island, which is protected by offshore rocks, is a 6-unit BC Forest campsite, heavily used by kayakers. Bring your own drinking water.

Tahsish and Kashutl Inlets and other places in Kyuquot Sound have limited unorganised camping opportunities—but sometimes you need the attitude of an East Indian saddhu to find them. Start looking early and don't be too picky.

### Distances
#### Within Kyuquot Sound
Fair Harbour to Artlish River – 5.5 nmi
Fair Harbour to Eelstow Passage – 4 nmi
Fair Harbour to Easy Inlet – 10 nmi
Fair Harbour to Tahsish River – 6.5 nmi
Fair Harbour to Hankin Cove – 6 nmi
Fair Harbour to Surprise Island – 8 nmi

#### On the Outside
Fair Harbour to Rugged Point – 11 nmi
Fair Harbour to Kyuquot – 12 nmi
Fair Harbour to Spring Island – 13.5 nmi
Fair Harbour to Bunsby Islands – 16 nmi
Fair Harbour to Jackobson's Point, South Brooks Peninsula – 27 nmi

# 29 Fair Harbour to Rugged Point

**Difficulty** Intermediate conditions – moderate risk.
**Distance** 11 nmi one way.
**Duration** 5-6 hours
**Chart** Kyuquot Sound No. 3682, 1:36,676, depth in fathoms
**Tides** on Tofino
**Currents** none

The fabulous sandy beaches accessible from a hiking trail beyond Rugged Point are the object of this somewhat dull approach. The journey is most enjoyable in the early morning before the wind rises.

### Paddling considerations

- Inflow-outflow winds are both predictable and to be avoided. Outflow winds blow up around 9 am (sometimes earlier) and continue till 4-6 pm.
- The long open spaces between the islands mean that the waves have space to build up quite a fetch.

- Inflow winds blow up after sundown sometimes drawing in thick offshore fog.
- Listen for high-speed power boats when entering or leaving the mouth of Fair Harbour.
- Few landing places let alone camp spots.
- Crossings
  – Fair Harbour launch to the first light beacon 1.3 nmi
  – Mainland to Whiteley Island 0.4 nmi

- Balcom Point to the mainland opposite 0.5 nmi.
- Sea fog toward Rugged Point
- No VHF reception for weather forecasts or assistance.

## The route

Avoid the boat launch ramp. It is apt to be busy with impatient fishing boats. Put in at one of the small rocky beaches east of it. Leave before 7 am to avoid the wind. In this area of potentially heavy traffic, pass approaching vessels port to port and listen carefully for fast running power boats when approaching the first and third light beacons in the exit to Fair Harbour.

---

### Amai Inlet

Amai Inlet, earlier known as Deep Inlet, was the site of mining operations in the 1940s. 457 metres above the ocean, miners sank three shafts in search of gold. They even set up a gondola to bring the ore out, but it didn't pay.

Ron Chidley, a gold miner's son, was one of five kids whose mother had lived all her life in the city of Toronto. The isolation of Amai Inlet and the fierce wild animals terrified her. The cougars got their dogs and cat. "One took the dog almost out from under Mom's feet," he said. She didn't know too much about geography so when the kids saw a sea lion, they used to tease her by saying that it was a crocodile. When she saw a heron, she didn't believe it was a bird because birds were not that big. To be safe, she locked all the kids in the house.

---

Sometimes paddlers take out at the Markale Indian Reserve No. 14 at the west end of Fair Harbour and portage across. It's quicker to paddle round instead of unpacking and re-packing unless you have four people to carry the loaded boats across with carrying straps. Homeward bound if wind is a problem, portaging can be useful. The Kyuquot Band ask that permission to camp be obtained beforehand. Respect the bears who consider the blackberries an important part of their fat build-up for winter.

Although Dixie Cove on Hohoae Island is a marine provincial park, it is very rocky and not suitable for camping. Unless the water is glassy smooth, don't cross over to it. Instead, follow the mainland south on the east side of Pinnace Channel. When you run out

---

### Cachalot Inlet

Between 1908 and 1926, Cachalot Inlet (then called Narrowgut Inlet) had a brief career as a whaling station. Five Norwegian-built whaling ships, each manned by eleven men, caught 400 whales a year. On shore, eighty men flensed the carcases and rendered the fat into oil which was exported to Proctor and Gamble in Cincinnati, Ohio for manufacturing soap.

The meat was shipped to California for fertiliser but during the first World War, 60,000 cases were canned for human food which was not popular. Whale meat tastes like tough beef sometimes with a fishy flavour.

In 1923, they found 537 lbs of ambergris in a sperm whale, a welcome bonus for a profitable industry.

*Launching backward into the surf.*

coast toward Rugged Point. Half-way there opposite Chatchannel Point, we stopped where an islet attached to the mainland by a rocky beach provided a temporary respite and a lunch spot. Hunkered down among the rocks we were able to nap in the warm sun out of the wind. An hour later, the wind seemed less fierce so we re-launched and made fine headway.

~

Approaching Rugged Point, the main camping area is where the provincial park sign is located just past Robin Point but there are other possibilities just before this.

~

*We arrived at Rugged Point to find two other groups there. A couple kayaking with a pair of dogs and a large group of experienced paddlers from Bellingham. They included Steve Schleicher, designer of Nimbus boats, and his partner, Jan Bain.*

*When I first met Steve, he was paddling a skinny banana boat on the Capilano River. Later he designed the Seafarer for himself. When others complained that it was too large, he downsized the design to produce the Solander and then a whole string of designs now afloat on three continents. He and Jan travel in a double and have learned to roll it consistently.*

*The group they were with had put in at the bridge over Little Espinosa Inlet, leaving one vehicle there and the rest at Fair Harbour. After a few soggy days on Catala Island, they paddled round Tatchu Point keeping over a mile offshore because of the boomers and up to Rugged Point. Off Mushroom Point, one of their number became seasick and had to be towed.*

of shoreline, cross to Whiteley Island and follow its shoreline past the fish farm to Balcom Point. Eat a snack and assess the weather beyond the point before venturing out. If you haven't been wearing your paddling jacket, you may want to put it on now. Look up into Amai and Cachalot inlets. Rocky and remote, they may be worth exploring if fog blankets your ongoing passage. The tiny cove at the entrance to Amai may contain pictographs.

From Balcom Point, cross over to the mainland watching for winds funnelling in or out of the two inlets. Paddle in a westerly direction following the shoreline until the bay before Rugged Point.

~

*At this point on one of my trips, the wind was beginning to get up so we set a due south course crossing quickly to the mainland and paddling along the*

# 30  Fair Harbour to Kyuquot

**Difficulty** Intermediate conditions – moderate risk
**Distance** 12 nmi one way.
**Duration** 5-6 hours
**Chart** Kyuquot Sound No. 3682, 1:36,676, depth in fathoms
**Tides** on Tofino
**Currents** none

An interesting but not spectacular trip best done before the winds come up.

## Paddling considerations

- Inflow-outflow winds are both predictable and to be avoided. Outflow winds blow up around 9 am (sometimes earlier) and continue until 4-6 pm.
- The long open spaces between the islands mean that the waves have space to build up quite a fetch.
- Inflow winds blow up after sundown sometimes drawing in thick offshore fog.
- Listen for high-speed power boats when entering or leaving the mouth of Fair Harbour.
- Few landing places let alone camping spots.

- Crossings
  - Fair Harbour launch to the first light beacon 1.3 nmi.
  - Markale Point to Hohoae Island 0.6 nmi.
  - Hohoae Island to Chutsis Island 0.8 nmi
  - Chutsis Island to the north end of Surprise Island 0.5 nmi
- Sea fog at the Kyuquot end can make it difficult to find one's way between the islands and into the settlement.

## The route

Be on the water by 7 am. Outflow winds blow up around 9 am (sometimes earlier) and continue till 4-6 pm. The long open spaces especially in Markale Passage can cause a nasty

fetch to build up. Listen for high-speed power boats when entering or leaving protected areas like the mouth of Fair Harbour or the channels around Surprise Island.

From the entrance to Fair Harbour, proceed south along the northern shore of Hohoae Island and cross to Chutsis Island, a small islet off the north shore of Union Island. If it's calm you may want to explore the south end of Hohoae Island.

If the wind continues to be a problem, cross to pass on the north side of Surprise Island for maximum shelter. The cove in behind Chutsis Island makes a good half-way stop. The upper part of Crowther Channel and the narrows behind Surprise Island are often quiet respites from the wind.

A few pilings are all that remain of the old Caledonia seal saltery just south of Surprise Island. During the 1939-45 world war, a family lived here untouched by the conflict.

From Caledonia down to Kyuquot, dodge in behind the headlands as much as possible. Once in the lee of Amos Island, the way into Kyuquot itself is fairly sheltered, but in fog don't follow the shoreline slavishly or you'll end up in the large basin of McKay Cove. When entering Kyuquot, watch for seaplanes pulling up to the government dock. Kayak landing is best done three or four houses west of the dock and then walk back along the trail.

*Caroline catches a snapper.*

# 31 Fair Harbour to the Artlish and Tahsish Rivers

**Difficulty** Intermediate conditions – moderate risk
**Distance** 5 nmi one way.
**Duration** 2-3 hours
**Chart** Kyuquot Sound No. 3682, 1:36,676, depth in fathoms
**Tides** on Tofino
**Currents** none

The Artlish River is an alternate launch used mainly by Kyuquot residents who keep their vehicles there.

The Tahsish River, which is protected by an ecological reserve, an Indian Reserve and a provincial park, was the beginning of one of two routes across Vancouver Island used by First Nations people. Both converge on Nimpkish Lake. In June 1862, Lt. Hankin traversed this route meeting his ship at Fort Rupert.

**Paddling considerations**
- Inflow-outflow winds
- Crossing. Fair Harbour launch to the first light beacon 1.3 nmi
- Outflow winds combined with a falling tide and the river's current can make the last part of this trip a hard paddle.

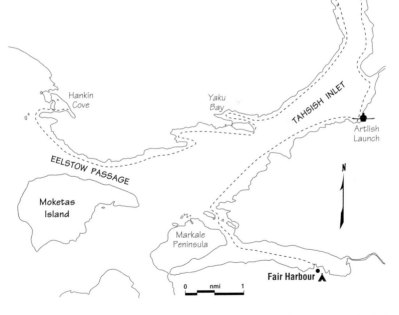

Both Tahsish and Tahsis come from the same Indian word tashee meaning trail or passage. First Nations people had two overland trails from the Tahsish River at the head of Kyuquot Sound and from the Tahsis River at the head of Tahsis Inlet. Both ended up at Nimpkish Lake and on down to Johnstone Strait.

• Mosquitoes and sweepers up the river.

## The Route

At the entrance to Fair Harbour, turn north up Tahsish Inlet. Follow the eastern shore on the way up past the Artlish River where most Kyuquot residents put in and take out. There are few landing places between here and the Tahsish River estuary. In the estuary, watch for sweepers and concealed rocks. The higher the tide, the easier the access.

Roosevelt elk were relocated to this area in the 1980s. At that time they were a rarity but since then they have been relocated to several other places like Sechelt and Powell River where they have multiplied and become more plentiful than planned. On a high tide, it's possible to get about a mile up the river.

The north side of the river mouth consists of Indian Reserve No. 11 and the south side of it is the Tahsish River Ecological Reserve. It was established in 1998 to protect an unaltered west coast estuary. This Reserve provides the primary access into the 11,022 hectare Tahsish-Kwois Provincial Park. The park encompasses the head-

*Tahsish River estuary.*

*Bird-like snags near Yaku Bay.*

waters of Kwois Creek, a tributary of the Tahsish River along with two lakes and a scenic river canyon. The old growth forest is one of the most important winter ranges for the elk on Vancouver Island. During salmon runs, bald eagles gather at the estuary to feast.

On the way back, follow the north-western shore of Tahsish Inlet and explore Yaku Bay, where once there was a saltery or cannery, and the following unnamed cove before continuing on through Eelstow Passage to perhaps stop at sheltered Hankin Cove.

~

*Returning from the Tahsish River, I noticed a weird and wonderful snag which looked like a half moon on top of a totem pole. It's a likely perch for a bald eagle or osprey though I saw neither at the time. In the unnamed cove south of Yaku Bay, Mew gulls and surfbirds had taken up residence on some floats.*

*Several of the shallow coves in Eelstow Passage contained large families of Common merganser chicks which ran on top of the water if I turned in toward them.*

*On one trip, two of us perched our tents on one of these beaches. The late night tide came within inches of my tent pole. Before this, we were rewarded by the sight of a minke whale surfacing with a big whoosh close by. We heard the same sound at our Easy Inlet camp and the crew of the Uchuck saw the whale in Chamiss Bay the previous week.*

## Overland Route

In 1862, Lt. Philip Hankin and Dr. C.B. Wood, RN of the British Admiralty survey ship *Hecate*, made two attempts to cross Vancouver Island from Kyuquot. The first attempt ended four miles up the Tahsish River in a downpour which, together with the rising river, was too much for his Kyuquot guides. Disappointedly they returned to Aktis where a guide more familiar with the route suggested they try again.

The rain had stopped so back they went making their first camp at the place where they had abandoned their first attempt, likely where Kwois Creek enters the Tahsish River. They hid the canoe in the bush and continued up the Tahsish valley on foot following well-trodden elk trails. The river had to be crossed several times but as the elk use gravel bars to cross, the fords were not too difficult to negotiate. The waterfalls and steep bluffs of the canyon area were more difficult. Hankin, who looked at the trees in terms of ship masts, reckoned they were 50-55 metres in height.

They built rafts of logs to traverse Atluk, Huston and Anutz Lakes. At Nimpkish Lake, they attached spars to form outriggers to a big log and, using a blanket, sailed and paddled the seventeen miles to the end of the lake where they hiked a trail down to Cheslakee, a Kwakwaka'wakw village on Johnstone Strait. From there a hired canoe took them to Fort Rupert to meet the Hecate.

*Mew gulls and surf birds near Yaku Bay.*

# 32 Fair Harbour to the head of Kashutl Inlet via Eelstow Passage, Hankin Cove and Easy Inlet

**Difficulty** Intermediate conditions – moderate risk
**Distance** 13.5 nmi one way.
**Duration** 5-6 hours
**Chart** Kyuquot Sound No. 3682 1:36,676, depth in fathoms
**Tides** on Tofino
**Currents** none

Caledonia Falls and the remains of a copper claim are at the head of Kashutl Inlet. On the way, Easy Inlet is sheltered water where yachts sometimes take refuge for a few quiet nights. Eelstow Passage is edged with little coves culminating in the well-hidden Hankin Cove.

**Paddling considerations:**
- Inflow-outflow winds
- Crossings
  – Fair Harbour launch to the inner light beacon 1.3 nmi
  – Markale Peninsula to McGrath Point, Moketas Island 0.7 nmi
  – Moketas Island to the beginning of Eelstow Passage 0.4 nmi
  – Expedition Islets to the west side of Kashutl Inlet 0.7 nmi
  – Mouth of Easy Inlet 0.4 nmi
- It's impossible to get a weather forecast on the VHF.
- The gravel quarry in Monteith Bay is noisy when in operation.

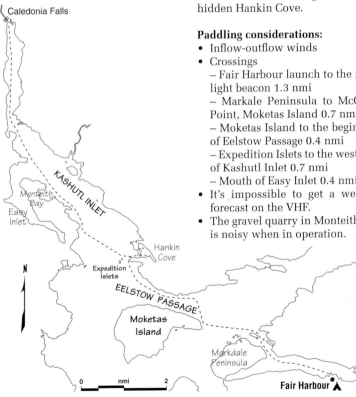

Caledonia Falls

KASHUTL INLET

Monteith Bay

Easy Inlet

Hankin Cove

Expedition Islets

N

EELSTOW PASSAGE

Moketas Island

Markdale Peninsula

Fair Harbour

0    nmi    2

## The route

From Fair Harbour, cross Tahsish Inlet to Moketas Island and then over to Eelstow Passage. Watch for a melanistic (dark) form of cougar. Twice they have been seen sitting on the rocks overlooking the passage. Cougars swim, so they could have just been wet.

Past the Expedition Islets where there may be seals look for the well-concealed entrance to Hankin Cove. This sheltered place is worth a visit especially if wind has been a problem.

~

*I approached Hankin Cove from the north and had to paddle almost all the way in before the entrance opened out in front of me. Once inside, a friendly seal greeted me and watched while I swam and ate lunch. I would have been happy to stay all day enjoying the sunshine and the peace.*

~

From Hankin Cove, continue up the eastern coast of Kashutl Inlet until it narrows south of Monteith Bay and then cross. The Bay contains a noisy gravel quarry so pass quickly and enter Easy Inlet which is sheltered from

### Head Of Kashutl Inlet

In 1919, J. Derberger and Charles G. Nordstrom filed copper claims at the head of Kashutl Inlet naming them Caledonia Falls Claims 1-14. They built several buildings one of which had a window looking directly down the 1.6 metre falls. This building was still standing in 1956 when Stan Sharcott took a prospector up there to re-evaluate the claims. As they hiked along the Kashutl River bank, Sharcott noticed some pink fawn lilies *Erythronium revolutum*. Native people used to boil the corms and serve them with oolichan grease. They always drank water afterwards to avoid getting sick.

the wind. Unfortunately, it may also have mosquitoes. Up at the head of Kashutl Inlet, Caledonia Falls drops 1.6 metres near the remains of a copper mine active in the early years of last century.

~

*We camped on a narrow stony beach near a creek at the entrance to Easy Inlet. The sun shone warmly on our fog-soaked clothes and we swam and washed our hair in the warm waters of the inlet. After the mosquitoes drove us into our tents, there was a loud whoosh outside. The next night when we heard the same noise in Eelstow Passage we saw a minke whale surface.*

### Easy Inlet

In 1913, prospectors found pyrophyllite at the entrance to Easy Inlet. They mined 120 tons of alunite which they vainly hoped would contain enough potash for fertiliser. All that remain are the shallow open cuts in the gravel.

Cement blocks and a few bricks mark a long gone saltery in the inlet. Now the occasional yacht arrives in search of sheltered anchorage.

# 33 Easy Inlet to Chamiss Bay and Kyuquot

**Difficulty** Intermediate – moderate risk
**Distance** 12 nmi one way.
**Duration** 4-5 hours
**Chart** Kyuquot Sound No. 3682, 1:36,676, depth in fathoms
**Tides** on Kyuquot
**Currents** none

An inlet paddle with the possibility of rendezvousing with the *Uchuck* at Chamiss Bay.

## Paddling considerations
- Inflow-outflow winds
- Crossings: Easy Inlet 0.4 nmi
- Sea fog toward Kyuquot

## The route
Cross Easy Inlet and hug the coast poking into all the indentations. Monteith Bay has an active gravel pit which is noisy. Some bays have cabins in them. Most are empty. There are a number of shingle beaches to land on if the wind gets up but not many camping places. Guillod Point is a good lunch spot. Watch for eagles on shore.

South of Guillod Point, Surprise Island narrows the waterway. Continue to hug the coast which becomes like a canal. Listen for power boats speeding through without expecting to meet anyone else. When Surprise Island falls away, the shoreline turns into a shallow bay with some pilings in a corner. Caledonia Seal Saltery operated here before World War II. In the late 1930s, the Hamilton family used some of the building lumber to construct a snug home where their children could grow up far from the sounds of war.

*Miss Charlie.*

A fish packer in the next bay runs a noisy generator. Continue for just over a nautical mile and round an unnamed point. Follow the coast for 0.6 nmi and you should see a port hand day marker in the distance. This is sheltered water so cross over to it watching and listening for seaplanes as you do so. When you see the village, look on the shore beside the port-hand day marker. Kyuquot's mascot, Miss Charlie, the seal, may be snoozing on the beach. This is one of her favourite places. Do not disturb her as she is very old.

### Miss Charlie

Esko Kayra, Miss Charlie's foster father, says she was 39 years old July 7, 2003. Her mother was shot before the seal pup was born by C-section. Esko's wife Lucy brought her up in the bathtub. When she first let her out to swim in the sea, she painted a white mark on her forehead so she wouldn't be shot. It wore off a long time ago and now everyone knows who she is especially as the restaurant (which is not open) is named after her. Now Miss Charlie swims where she wishes and is pleased to accept pelagic offerings from sport fishers. She often snoozes on the beach by the port-hand day marker at the east end of Walters' Island.

# 34 Rugged Point Beaches – as a hike

**Distance** 3 km one way
**Duration** 2-4 hours
**Chart** Kyuquot Sound No. 3682 1:36,676, depth in fathoms
**Tides** on Tofino

Three big glorious sandy beaches are the main attraction of Rugged Point.

A level hike after some rock scrambling to access the main beach

## The route

From the BC Parks campground at Rugged Point, follow the boardwalk past the biffy to the beach on the south side of the point. If you haven't been able to get a weather forecast in camp on the north side, you should be able to pull one in here.

Down on the beach, head east and climb a rocky point. At the top, an opening looks down onto logs washed up on the main beach, which you can't see. Go down this precipitous slope and out onto the beach.

Once past this obstacle, two large sandy beaches are spread out in front of you and a third is easily accessible just before Kapoose Creek. Allow at least a day to explore this area on foot. On the beaches, watch for cougar prints in the sand and look for fossils in the rocky limestone headlands separating the beaches. Near Kapoose Creek examine the border between forest and sand for the spiky prehistoric-looking heads of the Large-headed sedge, *Carex macrocephala.*

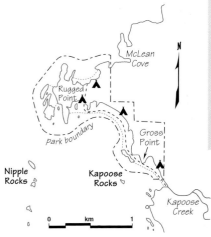

**First Nation's Currency**

Before Europeans arrived, Ehatisaht families had secret sources of money. One generation told the next which mountain peaks to line up with other landmarks so that a canoe could position itself exactly on top of beds of dentalia shells deep in the ocean. Using rakes of the tough twigs of Hardhack (*Spiraea douglasii*) the favoured few gathered the tiny, smooth, white tusk-like *Dentalium pretiosum* shell and threaded them into strings. A two-metre string bought a slave.

# 35 Rugged Point to Grassy Island

**Difficulty** Advanced conditions – considerable risk
**Distance** 3.5 nmi one way.
**Duration** 1-2 hours
**Chart** Kyuquot Sound No. 3682, 1:36,676, depth in fathoms
**Tides** on Tofino
**Currents** none

A sandy beach surmounted by a grassy knoll. Puffins can be seen on nearby Clark Island which is 0.5 nmi from Grassy Island and in the same island complex. On the way back, explore the big beaches south to Rugged Point.

## Paddling considerations

- Inflow-outflow winds
- Crossing. Mushroom Point to Clark 0.8 nmi
- The outer coast of Grassy Island is open to Pacific swells
- The landing place is approached from the northeast.
- Sea fog

## The route

From Rugged Point campsite, paddle out and round the point. Then head south dodging the boomers associated with the Nipple Rocks and Volcanic Islets to a largish island with a visible green area on it. This is Grassy Island. Come in through the reefs on the northeast side. There's a shell beach and good views up and down the coast. Since Grassy Island escaped the last ice age, it has a unique flora. Photograph but do not pick anything. The limestone rocks contain fossil shells similar to those found on the headlands separating the mainland beaches.

On a Thursday or Friday, the MV *Uchuck* will pass in the distance. Be prepared to overnight here if the weather changes

On leaving Grassy, head over to nearby Clark Island. Tufted puffins preen on its rocky ledges. Their large orange and yellow bills distinguish

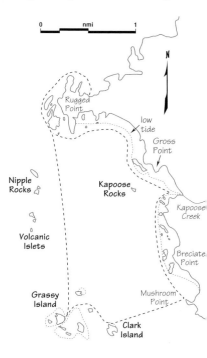

them from other birds. They moult the sheath every fall. Check anything with a fast wing beat. It could be a puffin or its near relative, a rhinocerous auklet. Keep 500 metres away during the nesting months of April to August.

From Clark Island, cross Clear Passage and work your way back up the coast to Rugged Point. Perhaps call in at Kapoose Creek for water or to see the Large-headed sedge *Carex macrocephala*. If the big "dog" print beside it lacks claw marks, it is likely a cougar print. Check the limestone rocks for fossils.

Try landing behind the reef at Gross Point. Camping is permitted above the high tide line behind the logs.

## Minke Whales

Minke whales *Balaenoptera acutorostrata* are the smallest of the baleen whales. They grow to about 10 metres long and live about 50 years. Isolated individuals are common in the coastal inlets where they feed on sandlance and schools of herring and other small fish. Dark on top and light underneath with a small dorsal fin near the tail. A white band often occurs across the pectoral flippers.

Watch for seabirds feeding on a herring ball. Sometimes Minkes will come up in the middle with their big mouths open, occasionally swallowing a bird.

*Landing on Grassy Island.*

# 36 Rugged Point to fresh water on Union Island.

**Difficulty** Intermediate conditions – moderate risk
**Distance** 1.6 nmi one way.
**Duration** 1/2 hour
**Chart** Kyuquot Sound No. 3682, 1:36,676, depth in fathoms
(Previously 3682, depth in fathoms)
**Tides** on Tofino
**Currents** none

Fresh water from a distant lake in the hills above and a waterfall.

## Paddling considerations:
- Watch the winds. A west wind combined with an ebb tide produces steep waves. Take lunch in case the winds blow up and possibly wait till evening to return.
- Crossing: 1.6 nmi
- Sea fog

## The route
On a compass heading of 320° magnetic, cross Kyuquot Channel and head north along the coast until a creek comes down. There is another creek in the next bay. This is a good place to practice compass crossings as you're not likely to miss Union Island. Most paddlers can follow such a course within five degrees either way. Yachts have about the same accuracy.

Take shampoo and laundry soap and plan a general clean-up.

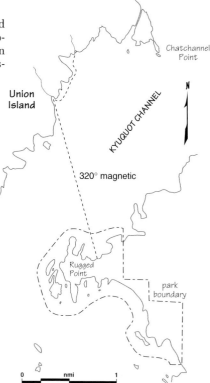

# 37 Rugged Point to Kyuquot

**Difficulty** Intermediate conditions – moderate risk
**Distance** 6.5 nmi one way.
**Duration** 2-3 hours
**Charts** Kyuquot Sound No. 3682, 1:36,676, depth in fathoms and Scoular Entrance and Kyuquot No. 3651, 1:7200, depth in metres
**Tides** on Tofino
**Currents** Confused water where the ebb tide from Kyuquot Channel meets the ocean.

This route goes along the south side of Union Island and Nicolaye Channel.

## Paddling considerations

- Inflow-outflow winds
- Crossings
  – Rugged Point light beacon to White Cliff Head 1 nmi
  – Entrance to Crowther Channel 0.5 nmi
- Sea fog

## The route

From Rugged Point, cross to White Cliff Head on Union Island and slip in behind the islands at the mouth of Kyuquot Bay. One or two have big shingle beaches which are nice to explore. Continue round the bay to Raccoon Point and then along the south shore of the island. On the west side of Union there are some small islands

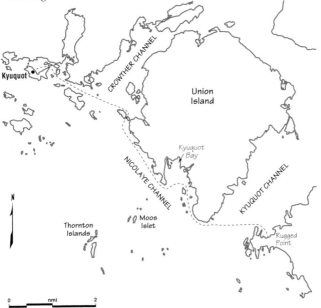

*Unnamed island in Kyuquot Bay.*

with places to land if the weather is bad. Cross Crowther Channel to Amos Island and paddle either side of it. The beacon on Rolston Island signals the entrance to Kyuquot harbour. Listen and watch for sea planes and fast moving power boats as you proceed. Chart No. 3651 is helpful for sorting out the islands.

# 38 Rugged Point to the Thornton Islands

**Difficulty**  Advanced conditions – considerable risk
**Distance**  4 nmi one way.
**Duration**  2-2 1/2 hours
**Chart**  Kyuquot Sound No. 3682, 1:36,676, depth in fathoms
**Tides**  on Tofino
**Currents**  none

A seldom-visited offshore island with a tiny cabin. It can be hazardous to reach and leave but it's worth the effort if your paddling skills are up to it. There's a good chance of seeing pelagic birds en route.

## Paddling considerations

- If gale force winds are predicted for the headlands, this counts as a headland.
- Crossings
  – Rugged Point light beacon to the Thornton Islands direct 3.5 nmi.
  – Rugged Point to White Cliff Head 1.1 nmi
  – Raccoon Point to Thornton Islands 1.9 nmi

- Experienced paddlers say this is often a fog crossing. Even if not, increasing wind may defer departure till next day. The cabin contains a note that one paddler was marooned there for a whole month in May
- Although the islands give minimal shelter from open ocean swells, paddlers encounter several large rock gardens of boomers which are hazardous.
- A tiny beach provides a safe surf-free landing at any height of tide.

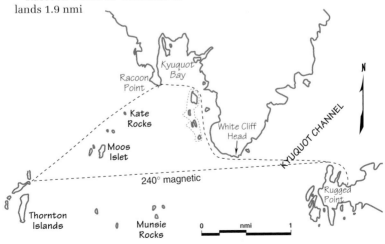

## The route

From Rugged Point, set a compass course of 240° magnetic. Watch for boomers during the last mile and a half. The course leads into the center bay of the three islets which make up the Thornton Islands. On the north side of this bay there is a tiny shingle cove where landing is easy at any tide.

An alternate route from White Cliff Head is to hug the inside of Kyuquot Bay to Raccoon Point. Keep north of Kate Rocks and Moos Islet (half-way but no landing) and continue on to the bay on the northeast side of the Thornton Islands. On this crossing, keep a sharp eye out for boomers and take evasive action. This requires concentration as the swells from the open Pacific are strong. If the wind freshens, listen to the forecast before leaving the islands and consider camping there overnight.

*We tried the direct route but found the seas too lumpy for our liking so we crossed over to White Cliff Head and ducked behind the islands in Kyuquot Bay at the south end of Union Island. On a previous trip we considered camping here but continued on to Spring Island after we watched a bear rub its back against a tree to mark it.*

*At Raccoon Point, we decided to try again. We fought our way out level with Moos Islet and then decided to go the whole way knowing that our friends had assured us that there was a safe landing. The waves were breaking occasionally and we got soaked around and over our spray skirts. Seals slithered off a rock which the surge tried to push us onto and a little later a flock of pelagic cormorants*

*Cabin on Thornton Island.*

*took off from a triangular rock which they had been adorning. After passing the rock, we headed for a grassy area on the north side of the Thorntons. As we got closer, we picked our way between the rocks till we saw a small beach with surf in front but it was only breaking over the guardian rocks. We slipped in behind them to find a green-lined pocket landing place. The rocks underfoot were slippery with weed.*

~

**On the Island**
Check the beaches for glass balls, and nesting gulls which should be left undisturbed. If the sea is calm enough it would be neat to paddle round some of the offshore rocks in search of puffins and other offshore birds such as Cassin's auklet and the ancient murrelet. Hike across the rocks to the cliff and use the thick grey plaited rope to scramble up the steep slope. Above is a tiny cabin, "Windy Villa" built in 1984 by members of the Whaletown Museum, Cortes Island. A note printed above the inside of the door says that "The natural history information gathered helps support the preservation of our wild places. Please send any interesting data to Box 83, Whaletown, Cortes Island." I got no answer to my letter to them but later was able to contact George Sirk, who built the cabin by e-mail. Another note requests: "Please leave the cabin a little tidier than when you found it." Elsewhere a note states that a paddler was marooned here for a month in May. A large container outside contains a turgid supply of water caught on the mossy cedar shingles of the roof. Two bunks and a stove complete the amenities. It would be good shelter in a storm but it is easier to camp on the beach. From the cabin, trails lead to high points from which glorious views up and down the coast spread out.

~

*Thankfully we landed and wrenched off our wet clothes. On the other side of the island whitecaps raged between us and Spring Island. As she changed, Caroline found a green glass roller float in a slimy pool at the back of the shingle and was delighted with her treasure.*

*Over lunch, we listened to the weather forecast which promised stronger winds and decided to wait till the four o'clock forecast. We were content to rest on land. In the shelter of*

*Glass roller float, Thornton Island.*

the rocks, the sun was hot. White gulls wheeled in the blue sky overhead. Two noisy oystercatchers screamed protest at our presence. Three sea otters played in the kelp.

Climbing up to the green marram grass, and looking north, I could see that the wind was escalating and even more whitecaps were breaking. A flock of California and Glaucous-winged gulls hunkered down on a nearby offshore rock. I longed to explore a guano-stained skerry farther out that might have had puffins on it but even the short trip there would have been hazardous.

"You have to go up to the cabin, it's easy," said Caroline who had already been so off I went while she swam and napped in the sun.

After scrambling over the rocks, I found the thick grey rope which led up to the cabin perched on top of the cliff. Two bunks, a stove, a wash basin, a water catchment system into a noxious black cistern. A notepad in a plastic bag contained the news that another paddler had visited that very morning. Perhaps it was he who left several packets of dried food in another plastic bag. Will the mice have a feast? I too left a note and then climbed up the hill to the south where I enjoyed the view down to Tatchu and Ferrer Points and took some photographs.

The 4 pm forecast was no better so we decided to camp. The wind was so strong that our tents acted like kites. We threw heavy bags into them *before lashing them down with rocks and logs buried in the shingle. After supper, I practiced my Tai Chi on a tiny, sunny shell beach while Caroline searched for a vantage point from which to watch the sunset. There she found a large fluffy gull chick. It may have been the one that later squawked around my tent in the wee hours of the night.*

*Waking at midnight, the wind had died. A large yellow planet, which I later found to be Mars, shone over the mountains at Rugged Point and was reflected in the water like a second moon. At 5 am, I listened to the forecast again—gale warning 15-25 knot winds rising to 30 knots in the afternoon. All was still so we rose, packed and had a hurried breakfast. Watched by a solitary Willet, we departed at 7 am.*

~

If you're lucky enough to be there in calm weather and can paddle round the outer skerries, there are several narrow channels between them. The 10 metre-wide and 80 metre-long one on the southwest side of the island is called The Shute according to George Sirk. He used to take his Zodiac through it at high tide. "There is a rock to watch out for on the south side mid channel," he says.

Be careful not to go so close to birds on ledges that they fly off. Nesting on a ledge often requires the bird to face inward against the rock, just to stay in place. If they leave even for a moment, hungry predators such as glaucous-winged gulls, eagles and ravens swoop down to steal the eggs or the chicks. Ocean birds don't lay a second clutch if disaster strikes the first.

*Mainland (Rugged Point) from Thornton Islands.*

# 39 Thornton Islands to Spring Island

**Difficulty** Advanced conditions – considerable risk
**Distance** 4 nmi one way.
**Duration** 1-2 hours
**Chart** Kyuquot Sound No. 3682, 1:36,676, depth in fathoms
**Tides** on Tofino
**Currents** none

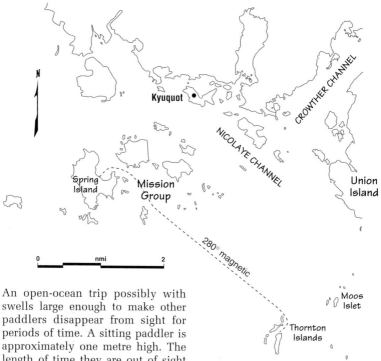

An open-ocean trip possibly with swells large enough to make other paddlers disappear from sight for periods of time. A sitting paddler is approximately one metre high. The length of time they are out of sight gives an idea of the swell height. A few shallow points visible on the chart may increase the height of the waves and even cause them to break. Avoid these.

En route watch for murres and other pelagic birds.

Pelagic birds spend most of their lives away from land. For a better chance of seeing them, hire a boat to take you farther offshore than most kayaks care to go. However, on any open-ocean trip keep an eye out for the following:

– Sooty and Short-tailed shearwaters (*Puffinus griseus* and *Puffinus tenuirostris*) Brown birds with wingspans of 38-40" which skim over the tops of the waves.

– Pink-footed shearwaters (*Puffinus creatopus*). Brown birds with white stomachs and a wingspan of 43"

– Leach's Storm-petrel (*Oceanodroma leucorhoa*). Small brown birds with wingspans of 20" which dart back and forth like swallows, When feeding, they "foot-patter" on top of the water.

– Black-footed albatross (*Phaebastria nigripes*). A large dark bird with a wingspan of 84". Usually these are farther offshore.

None of these birds are common and most are solitary. They have a stiff wing beat followed by gliding with their wings in an anhedral (drooped) position. See also the sidebar on salt glands on page 142.

Another bird which is more often seen on water than on land is the Common murre (*Uria aalge*). These black birds with white shirt fronts are the North American equivalent to the penguin. You almost always see small flocks of them on open water crossings. Scientists have documented murre dives of up to 100 fathoms.

## Paddling considerations

- Inflow-outflow winds
- Crossing.Thornton Islands to Favourite Entrance 2.6 nmi
- Mark the appropriate compass course on each paddler's chart before leaving in case fog swirls in and verbally remind each other of the heading to be followed.
- Before heading out, plan what to do if the wind freshens or switches.
- Verbally review rescue procedures and discuss what the group would do if one person capsized in 2 metre waves. Remind paddlers not to get too close or too far away in these conditions.
- Be prepared to stay extra nights or return to Union Island and proceed to Spring Island via Kyuquot.

### The route

Set a course of 280° for the entrance to Favourite Entrance on the south side of Spring Island and keep paddling swell by swell until just past the first sheltering rocky islets. If the swells start to break, keep the momentum up by paddling hard. Surfers often take waves over their heads with no problem. If necessary lean into the wave, never away from it. Bang the paddle on the top or stick it into the middle. Brace if necessary. Don't worry about a wet spray skirt or arms. Forget trying to take photographs.

Once in the shelter of the Mission Group, only land on Spring. Aktis was the main village of the Kyuquot people and some of the elders still live there in seclusion. Kamils is a burial island that no one is allowed to land on. The north side of the sheltered inner bay of Spring contains Rupert

*Landing on Spring Island. Mount Paxton erosion in the background.*

Wong's West Coast Expeditions Camp. Look for camp spots on the south side or on the outer southern beaches of the island. A well-used trail crosses the island to the remains of a World War II defence. Some of the beaches in this area have large tide pools, well worth exploring possibly with snorkel equipment.

### Salt Glands

Birds which live their lives at sea have to be able to survive without fresh water. They manage even though sea water is three times saltier than their body fluids. A special gland behind their bill and above their eyes removes the excess salt from their blood and excretes it as a waste fluid. It either drips off the end of their bills as in gulls and ducks or out of a short separate tube located above their bills. This is why shearwaters and other oceanic birds are called tubenoses.

# 40 Kyuquot to Spring Island

**Difficulty** Beginner conditions – low risk
**Distance** 2 nmi one way.
**Duration** 1 hour
**Charts** Kyuquot Sound No. 3682, 1:36,676, depth in fathoms and Scoular Entrance and Kyuquot No. 3651, 1:7200, depth in metres
**Tides** on Tofino
**Currents** none

An easy crossing to the Mission Group of Islands of which Spring is one.

## Paddling considerations

- Inflow-outflow winds from McKay Cove and Crowther Channel
- Crossing. Nicolaye Channel 0.6 nmi
- Sea fog—Beginners should stay on shore

## The route

Paddle either side of Walter's Island and round to the centre of it. Cross Nicolaye Channel to the east end of Ahmacinnit Island and enter the sheltered waters of Barter Cove. The Kyuquot people do not want paddlers to land on Aktis or Kamils. Continue past them and veer west round Aktis. Toward the end of it, the island opposite it is the inside of Spring (See also Trip 41).

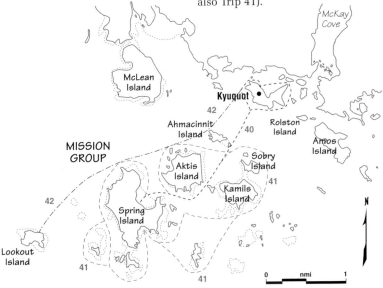

# 41 Circumnavigation of Spring Island and the Mission Group

**Difficulty** Advanced conditions – considerable risk (on the outside)
**Distance** 3-6 nmi one way.
**Duration** 2-4 hours
**Chart** Kyuquot Sound No. 3682, 1:36,676, depth in fathoms
**Tides** on Tofino
**Currents** none
**Map** See map for Trip 40

A mixture of very sheltered water and very open ocean. The main attractions are the historical significance of the Mission Group, the deep tide pools accessible from the outer beach on Spring Island, and the possibility of seeing pelagic birds off the outer coast.

## Paddling considerations

- On-shore, off-shore winds
- Crossings. Sheltered waters between the islands
- Landing is not allowed except on Spring Island.
- Sea fog—could make avoiding boomers difficult

## The route

Assuming a starting point from a campsite on the inside of Spring Island, assess the weather before deciding whether to tackle the inside or the outside first. If the weather is good, take the outside but keep an eye out for change. In case of emergency, there is a well-travelled trail across the island from the remains of the Loran Station back to the inside bay on the north side.

*Caroline contemplating Favourite Entrance, Mission Group.*

*Kayaks on South Beach, Spring Island.*

The tide pools are deep enough to snorkel in. Fronds of surf grass clothe the sides often concealing giant green sea anemones. Nearby shell beaches are composed of blue mussel shells. Although Japanese oysters were introduced to the area, they did not thrive because the water is not calm enough.

On the inside, paddle around but do not land on the other islands. Kyuquot elders living on Aktis wish to enjoy their ancient homeland undisturbed and the islands of Kamils, Sobry and Ahmacinnit are burial places. For details see sidebar: Kyuquot's Last Great War on page 112.

En route, you may meet guided parties from West Coast Expeditions. These are often people with no kayaking experience at all so do not follow them or tempt them to follow you. If necessary, escort them back to the guide who is likely searching for them.

# 42 Kyuquot to Lookout Island

**Difficulty** Advanced conditions – considerable risk
**Distance** 3.5 nmi one way.
**Duration** 1-2 hours
**Chart** Kyuquot Sound No. 3682 1:36,676, depth in fathoms
**Tides** on Tofino
**Currents** none
**Map** See map for Trip 40

An often missed island, but on a calm day, you might see pelagic birds on the ocean side.

## Paddling considerations

- On-shore, off-shore winds
- Crossings
  - Nicolaye Channel 0.7 nmi
  - Spring Island to Lookout Island 0.8 nmi
- Ocean swells
- Sea fog
- Rocky landing

## The route

From Kyuquot, cross Nicolaye Channel heading for Gayward Rock and the west side of the Mission Group. Stay on the outside of Aktis and Spring. Cross over to the north east end of Lookout Island where there is a rough landing place. Ashore there is no salal, just sedges to your knees under a canopy of Sitka spruce. On the outer coast of the island look for pelagic birds both on the rocks and on the offshore waves. Heerman's gulls often hang out on rocky shores like this.

*Leo Jack's water taxi service.*

# 6

# Bunsby Islands and South Brooks Peninsula

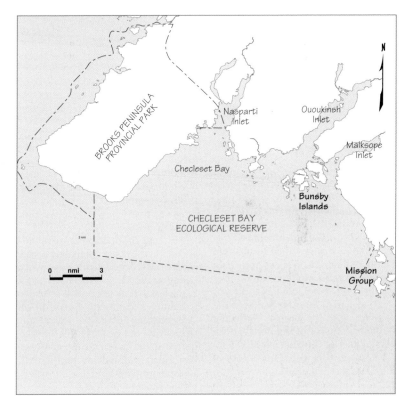

*Bunsby Island sunset.*

Sooner or later, most west coast paddlers look longingly at the mecca of the Brooks Peninsula. Because of the winds, most don't get much farther than the campsites at Jackobson Point, which are beautiful enough to satisfy them.

In a northwest wind, those who continue find the southern coast fairly sheltered until Clerke Point. There the land mass of the peninsula causes the already strong winds to channel round it increasing in speed as they do so. In rare calm weather, some lucky paddlers reach Solander Island.

Almost all of this area is within the boundaries of the Brooks Peninsula Provincial Park, the Big Bunsby Provincial Park or the Checleset Ecological Reserve. It is also the territory of the Checleset People.

In 1969, sea otters were re-introduced from Alaska and have since spread as far south as Nootka Island. It was to protect them that the Checleset Ecological Reserve was established. Although they can be seen at many other places up and down the coast, their presence is what primarily draws so many paddlers to the Bunsby Islands.

Although the main points of interest are out on the ocean, the inlets behind can be useful refuges in case of fog. Unfortunately, most have been logged in the last twenty years so don't expect too much old growth forest. If you carry a fishing license, try clam digging at low tide but be careful to fill your holes back in as you go and don't take any undersized shells so that there will be more for the future. Garlic butter is a great accompaniment.

## Launches

See Kyuquot Sound
Water taxi from Kyuquot

## Camping Locations

For permission to camp, call in at the Band Office before leaving Kyuquot. Out in the Bunsby's, Elder Lucy Paivio, who lives on Checkaklis Island by Green Head, can advise you. She is the Checleset Chief's sister and has authority to speak for him. Consult her for areas between the Bunsby Islands and right out to the Brooks Peninsula. Her up-to-date local knowledge is a treasure.

### Big Bunsby Island

Although BC Parks have not developed campsites, they say there are plenty of places to set up camp on this island. It can be crowded.

### Battle Bay

Away from Indian Reserve No.3, there is good beach camping here and also water from the creek by the reserve.

### Jackobson Point

The sheltered cove behind the Point, called Peddlar's Cove also has good camping. A very rough trail, which would be difficult to portage, crosses the point to more camping opportunities on the outer beach where a surf landing is required.

## Checleset People

The Checleset People were renowned as great songsters living in a land of flowers and berries. Commercial fishing drew their people to spend more and more time in Kyuquot. Eventually the few who remained left after their chief died in a tragic shooting accident. Their descendants, though still maintaining their ancestral heritage for ceremonial purposes, have amalgamated with the Kyuquot Band for convenience. Checleset elder, Lucy Paivio lives in the Bunsby Islands keeping an eye on things. She welcomes visitors.

Among their legends one describes a ship full of Europeans arriving but not landing. Some say this was Perez aboard the *Santiago* but the general opinion is that his encounter occurred off the Hesquiat Peninsula. Perhaps it was another Spanish ship which the Checlesets met. Joseph Ingraham visited Kyuquot in the brigantine *Hope* 1790-92. The answer may be lost among the secrets in the archives in Madrid as Spain saw no reason to tell the world what her explorers found.

The main winter Checleset village of Acous was on Battle Bay and the summer one, Upsowis, was near the west entrance to Malksope Inlet. This was better positioned for fishing and the summer hunting of seals and sea lions on the O'Leary Islets. A number of other villages up Malksope and Ououkinsh Inlets were used during fishing seasons for sockeye, coho, dog salmon and halibut.

# 43 Kyuquot to the Bunsby Islands

**Difficulty** Advanced conditions – considerable risk
**Distance** 8 nmi one way.
**Duration** 3 hours
**Chart** Checleset Bay No. 3683, 1:36,493, depth in fathoms
**Tides** on Tofino
**Currents** none

The most hazardous part of getting to the mecca of the Bunsby Islands.

## Paddling considerations

- Inflow-outflow winds
- Crossings
  – McLean Island to Malksope Point 5 nmi.
  – Mouth of Malksope Inlet 0.6 nmi

- Open ocean swells
- Sea fog. Set compass course before leaving
- Inhospitable rocky coast. The only landing between McLean Island and Malskope Point is out at Thomas Island. May be too rocky at low tide.

## The route

Leave by the west side of Walter's Cove and paddle along the coast. The first cove is called Olebar's Lagoon. Entry depends on the tide to float you over some slippery rocks. Past Olebar's, the big cove before McLean Island is Clanninick. This is an ecological reserve protecting a small, exceptional stand of old growth Sitka spruce. Look but continue on your way.

Come round the outside of McLean Island and assess the situation. If it's not favourable, retreat and try again later. (Although you can't camp in Clanninick Cove, a BC Parks map notes an unorganised campsite just west of

McLean Island. Although I've asked a lot of people about it, no one seems to remember it, possibly because it is not a very good one. Some maps mark campsites where none exist or where there's only room for one tent.)

Beyond this point, it's a two hour crossing with almost no shelter from the distant skerries on the ocean side. At mid tide, people have scrambled ashore at Thomas Island which is bisected by a sheltered canal. At low tide, this may be too rocky to land. The first real shelter and a possible camp spot is in behind Malkscope Point. Along the way, there are intriguing caves in the rocks but backwash from the cliffs may prevent a close examination of them. Keep an eye out for pelagic birds.

In 1992, National Geographic published a horrendous picture of Mount Paxton showing a very bad example of erosion caused by a logging road. Actually, there was more too it than that. Fire got away and raged to the mountain top. The ensuing uproar, and much lobbying by Kyuquot residents Sam Kayra and Cindy Lee, caused changes to the way logging roads were built in subsequent years throughout the province. After a clearcut, it takes about 3 years for the land to green over which, to some extent, this has done.

There is water at Malkscope Point and none on the Bunsby's so fill up. The main campsite is on Big Bunsby, the biggest island which is east of Gay Passage. Many kayakers hire a Kyuquot water taxi to bring them out here so expect to meet others. Although Checkaklis Island may be visited, camping is not allowed. Overuse

### Elder Lucy Paivio's Message

"I ask of the visitors who come to enjoy the beauty of our land and sea, please do not upset or damage them during your visit. Someone may be coming today to see what you took yesterday. Our people have all learned a hard lesson from history. Let us all learn a lesson from this and approach with clear minds, your reasons for coming to our Checleset Kyuquot Territory. And ensure they are such that the beauty remains to share for a long time to come."

prompted this 1994 decision by the hereditary chief of the area. Please respect it.

### In the Bunsby Islands.
Explore the large island west of Gay Passage. In the canal which almost bisects it is a fish weir. Go ashore and visit Elder Lucy Paivio at her cabin on Checkaklis Island. She is the chief's sister and welcomes visitors. Ask to climb up to the lookout near Green Head from where there is a great view of the Brooks Peninsula. Also, ask her about going over to Acous to see the totem poles and the canoe graves. As a thank you for her hospitality, take her some fresh fruit, vegetables or chocolate and ask to see her weaving which she sells.

While paddling around the islands, keep a sharp eye out for sea otters and enjoy them at a distance. Don't approach crying pups which the mother often parks in the kelp. She may be afraid to come back while you are around.

# 44 Malksope Inlet

**Difficulty** Intermediate conditions – moderate risk
**Distance** 5 nmi one way.
**Duration** 2 hours
**Chart** Checleset Bay No. 3683, 1:36,493, depth in fathoms
**Tides** on Tofino
**Currents** none

Malksope Inlet is seldom paddled because it has been scarred by logging and is unexpectedly windy. The most attractive points of interest are at its entrance: the old Checleset winter village of Upsowis and whales.

## Paddling considerations

- Katabatic/anabatic winds inside
- Crossing. Mouth of Malksope Inlet 0.6 nmi
- Once inside the inlet, you may lose the fog.

## The route

Paddle up one side of the inlet and back down the other. Twenty years ago and more, the inlet was used to assemble log booms before taking them south. The remains of this activity can still be seen along the shore. It's a typical fjord with katabatic/anabatic winds whistling down its steep slopes. The northwest corner has a very large clearcut and unravelling slope which is unattractive. At the head, two logging roads follow each side of the Malksope River. The northerly one

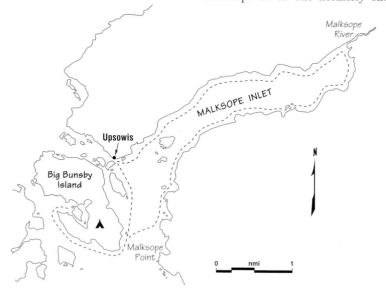

*Elephant seal. Photo: Martin Kafer.*

goes 13 km to the head of Ououkinsh Inlet and the southerly one 18 km to Chamiss Bay where the *Uchuck* calls in early on Friday mornings.

At the entrance explore the old Checleset winter village of Upsowis whose wind-blown trees resemble a Japanese garden. The locals sometimes call it Hollywood because a movie was shot here but no one remembers the title. The water here is poorer quality than that at Izard Point in nearby Ououkinsh Inlet.

An upwelling in the water at the entrance to Malksope and round into the southeaster part of Checleset Bay attracts whales to the area. This is the best place to see humpback, minke and orca along with harbour porpoise.

### Elephant Seals

If you see a very large seal with a bashed in face, it is probably an elephant seal *Mirounga angustirostris*. Males grow 4 metres long and weigh up to 2000 kgs Non-breeding elephant seals are seen regularly in British Columbia waters. Nuchatlitz residents have seen them occasionally. If you see what appears to be a dead head or a floating barrel, look closer, it might be an elephant seal dozing on the surface slowly going up and down.

# 45  Bunsby Islands to the Acous Peninsula (Battle Bay)

**Difficulty**  Advanced conditions – considerable risk
**Distance**  2-3 nmi one way.
**Duration**  1-2 hours
**Chart**  Checleset Bay No. 3683, 1:36,493, depth in fathoms
**Tides**  on Tofino
**Currents**  none

This trip goes into the heart of Checleset Territory where it is important to respect any relics found.

## Paddling considerations

- Inflow-outflow winds
- Crossing. Gay Passage to the Skirmish Islands 1.6 nmi
- Open ocean swells
- Sea fog. Set compass course before leaving.

## The route

From Gay Passage, head across the mouth of Ououkinsh Inlet to the Skirmish Islets. In Battle Bay, go ashore to beachcomb, collect water or camp.

On the outer coast of the Acous Peninsula, there is an old village site where totem poles peak out of the vegetation. Don't miss exploring the tiny Cuttle Islets which could easily take all day.

One of the outer islands has a moss-covered canoe burial. Be careful where you step and look but do not touch. There is also a 1997 boat burial there too.

Cross Ououkinsh Inlet back to the Bunsby Islands and dally awhile exploring them. Circumnavigate Checkaklis Island to see Green Head, a rock which resembles its name. Call in to meet Elder Lucy Paivio on Checkaklis Island if she's home. Take some fresh fruit, vegetables or chocolate to thank her for her stories. She also sells her weaving.

# 46 Ououkinsh Inlet

**Difficulty** Intermediate conditions – moderate risk
**Distance** 6-7 nmi one way.
**Duration** 2-3 hours
**Chart** Checleset Bay No. 3683, 1:36,493, depth in fathoms
**Tides** on Tofino
**Currents** none

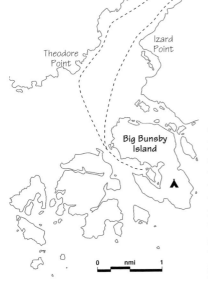

Adventurous souls paddle up the inlet and then up the Power River to the lake but the last bit is tough going. For more laid-back paddlers, the water at Izard Point is good and there may be clams in the protected cove at the head of the inlet. Often sail boats anchor here. The logging road on the south side of this cove, runs for 13 km to the head of Malksope Inlet and then a farther 18 km to Chamiss Bay where the *Uchuck* calls in early on Friday mornings.

## Paddling considerations

- Inflow-outflow winds
- Crossing. Izard Point to the northwest side of Ououkinsh Inlet is 0.6 nmi
- Very little boat traffic
- Once past the entrance, you may lose the sea fog.

## The route

Proceed up one side and down the other. This inlet is less sheltered than Malksope so keep an eye on the weather. Beyond the Hisnit Islands, the Power River flows down from a nearby lake of the same name. It used to be easy to hike along an old logging road which followed the river bank to the lake but that has quite over grown now. Instead, line your boat up the river at high tide and walk the

*Green Head, Bunsby Islands.*

rest of the way. A short box canyon backwaters the lake. Swim through it till it opens out. Energetic paddlers who drag their boats all the way in can paddle to the end of the lake and camp on a large alluvial fan.

The Checleset had summer fishing villages at the mouths of both the Power and the Ououkinsh Rivers. Likely they dug clams as well. The chart marks three large areas which dry at low tide. Try them if you remembered to check in Kyuquot to see if there is a Paralytic Shellfish Poison (P.S.P.) warning.

### Peddlar's Cove Wreck

Leo Jack says that some years ago a handlogger bought an old boat off the Coast Guard for $1.00. He towed it to Peddlar's Cove intending to use it as a cabin. One day when he was away a big storm blew up and drove it ashore where it still lies. He never returned.

# 47 Battle Bay to Jackobson Point

**Difficulty** Advanced conditions – considerable risk
**Distance** 12 nmi one way.
**Duration** 4-5 hours
Chart Checleset Bay No. 3683, 1:36,493, depth in fathoms
**Tides** on Tofino
**Currents** none

At last, the Brooks Peninsula! This is as far as most paddlers go.

## Paddling considerations
- Inflow-outflow winds
- Crossings
  - Mainland to Scarf Island 0.5 nmi
  - Scarf Island to the mainland 2 nmi
- Open ocean swells
- Sea fog. Set compass course before leaving
- Surf landing on the beach west of Jackobson Point. Calm on the inner east side.

## The route
From Battle Bay, round the Acous Peninsula and follow the mainland coast on the inside of a couple of unnamed islands. The second one is joined to the mainland by a spit, so try to be there at high tide or go round it. The neighbouring islands will still provide some shelter. From the end of the last one, cross to Scarf Island and then to the mainland. Proceed west along the shore till the island before Jackobson Point. Behind it is Peddlar's Cove, sometimes called Columbia Cove, a favourite shelter for fishing boats. This is also a good campsite with a trail across the peninsula to a beautiful outer surf beach.

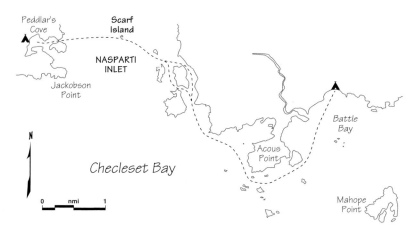

# 48 Jackobson Point to Johnson Lagoon and the head of Nasparti Inlet

Difficulty Intermediate conditions – moderate risk
Distance 5 nmi one way.
Duration 2-3 hours
Chart Checleset Bay No. 3683, 1:36,493, depth in fathoms
Tides on Tofino
Currents tidal current in the entrance to Johnson Lagoon.

A trip to try if you're waiting to cross Nasparti Inlet to return to Acous, but take overnight gear in case weather or tide strands you. With care, it could also be done in fog with the added bonus that once inside the lagoon, the fog might dissipate and there's a pretty trip up the Nasparti River.

**Paddling considerations**
- Inflow-outflow winds
- Crossings: none
- Sea fog at the entrance to Nasparti Inlet

**The route**
From Peddlar's Cove paddle north up Nasparti Inlet. Getting in and out of Johnson Lagoon is a matter of timing. The chart has the notation: "At springs, slack water is two hours after

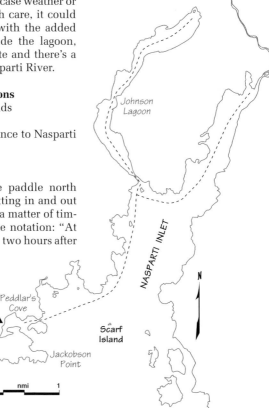

*Butter Clams ready for the pot.*

high water and 2 ½ hours after low water." Plan accordingly. There is a six foot tidal drop. Once in, you'll have to wait to get out. The lagoon was logged using an A-frame in the 1970s and is still struggling to recover so the trees are secondary growth. The three creek estuaries on the west side are possible landing places. At the head of the lagoon, there is a historic trail providing access to the upper reaches of the Nasparti River.

If you've arrived at the wrong time, continue up to the head of Nasparti Inlet. There are some interesting coves and a big sandbar and lagoon at the end. If you arrive just before high high water, you can paddle about a kilometre up the river which is wild and beautiful. Don't stay long or be prepared to drag your boats over slippery rocks on the way back. Wildlife trails on either side of the river are not particularly easy to use but are the best foot access. An anchor on the chart at the head of the inlet means that the water is fairly sheltered from the prevailing winds but it won't be if a southwester blows.

If paddling at dawn or dusk, watch for Roosevelt elk especially near fresh water. This is one of their favourite haunts on Vancouver Island.

# 49 Brooks Peninsula: Jackobson Point to Solander Island

**Difficulty** Advanced conditions – considerable risk
**Distance** 11.6 nmi one way
**Duration** 6 hours one way in perfect weather and sea conditions
**Charts** Checleset Bay No. 3683, 1:36,493, depth in fathoms and Nootka Sound to
  Quatsino Sound No. LC 3604, 1:150,000, depth in metres
**Tides** on Tofino
**Currents** none

The real diehards will want to do this just to say they've been even though they need a permit and rock climbing skills to land on Solander.

## Paddling considerations

- Winds increase as they funnel round the peninsula
- 15 knots more wind out at Solander Island.
- Crossing: mainland to Solander Island 0.9 nmi
- Surf landings
- Have lunch reachable in your boat as you won't be able to land.
- Be able to pee in your boat.

- Sea conditions are often too hazardous for a water taxi to get in to rescue you from the beaches beyond Clerke Point.
- Perfect weather and sea conditions might last the six hours or so to reach Solander, but will they last long enough for the return journey?
- Peddlar's Cove, behind Jackobson's Point, is the only safe haven from a storm on the south side of the Brooks Peninsula.
- Camping is possible on some of the surf beaches but be prepared to be stormbound for several days.

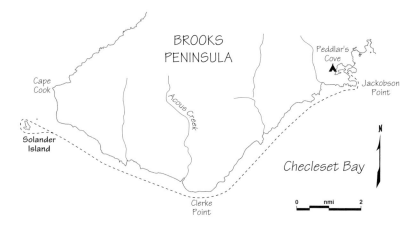

*West side of Solander island. Photo: Ann Cooper.*

## The route

Round Jackobson Point and continue west along the peninsula. All the beaches along here require surf landings and you could be storm stayed on them. Reefs, called the Shelter Sheds, extend out from the coast and provide a popular shelter for fishing boats especially when the wind is from the northwest. In southerly winds, surf landings become the norm.

A small Indian Reserve with a tiny cabin is tucked in to a small cove immediately east of Clerke Point. It's a potential landing place.

At Clerke Point, an extensive shingle bar stretches out from the shore. Beyond here, the weather and sea conditions can change radically.

For those fortunate enough with the weather to want to proceed, change charts. Small groups of pad-dlers have camped at the unnamed creek which comes down in the centre of the nose of the peninsula. It is 2.2 nmi from Clerke Point. Be prepared to be stormbound here.

Solander Island, off the north end of the Brooks Peninsula, is known for its confused seas where two sets of waves meet, and its extreme weather. Winds round the island may be 15 knots more than either close to the peninsula or farther offshore. Its rocky shores discourage landing and besides, it's an ecological reserve which is closed to the public. To reach it, paddle 2.5 nmi north and then cross 0.9 nmi to the island. Circumnavigate, but plan to return to the mainland to land.

For botanical enthusiasts, hike up Amos Creek, immediately north of Clerke Point to search out unglaciated Alpine plants and enjoy stupendous

## Solander Island

Solander Island is an eight hectare ecological reserve that is closed to the public to avoid disturbing the birds. The island is an important international breeding area for the blue-listed Tufted puffin (*Fratercula cirrhata*) and Cassin's auklet (*Ptychoramphus aleuticus*) and yellow-listed species of conservation concern (S4) Pelagic cormorant (*Phalacrocorax pelagicis*). It has the third largest Leach's storm petrel (*Oceanodroma leucorhoa*) colony on the B.C. coast.

In winter, red-listed Northern (Stellar) sea lions (*Eumetopias jubatus*) haul out on its rocky shores and sea otters are seen in its surrounding kelp beds.

The island is devoid of trees. It is one of only six locations in the province where the blue-listed Hairy goldfields (*Lasthenia maritima*) is found.

The weather station, which is unmanned, is on top and is accessed by helicopter.

views. Landing may be difficult. Leo Jack has had problems getting people in with his water taxi. He thinks some paddlers who have gone up the river at high tide may have camped there. At low tide the creek disappears under the beach.

~

*Ann Cooper and five friends camped a couple of nights at the end of the Brooks Peninsula in 1995. The weather was calm so they paddled out and round Solander Island. They didn't notice any landing places. Two years later, Cooper paddled down from Winter Harbour with a SKABC group and circumnavigated the island again. On the way back they noticed a small emergency "bolt hole" just east of Cape Cook on the north side of the Brooks. It is rare to be this lucky with the weather twice. In August 2003, two veteran west coast paddlers poked their bows round Clerke Point and retreated quickly not liking the sea conditions. This is more normal.*

# Useful Contacts

## Nootka Sound

### Ahaminaquus Tourist Centre,[12]
P.O. Box 1137,
Gold River, BC
V0P 1G0
Phone 1-800-238-2933

### Air Nootka
P.O. Box 19,
Gold River, BC
V0P 1G0
Tel: (250) 283-2255
Fax: (250) 283-2256

### Critter Cove Marina
P.O. Box 1118,
Gold River, BC
V0P 1G0
Tel/Fax: (250)283-7364
www.crittercove.com

### Gold River Visitor's Bureau,
Box 610,
Gold River, BC
V0P 1G0
Tel: (250) 283-2418 or
(250) 283-2202

### Maxi's Water Taxi & Charter Service,[14]
P.O. Box 1122,
Gold River, BC
V0P 1G0
Tel: (250) 283-2282
Fax: (250) 283-2335

### Moutcha Bay Marina
E-mail: info@moutchabay.com
Tel: (250) 923-2980
www.moutchabay.com

### Nootka Sound Services Ltd. (MV Uchuck)
P.O. Box 57,
Gold River. BC
V0P 1G0
Tel: (250) 283-2515
Fax: (250) 283-7582
www.mvuchuck.com

### Tuta Marina
Larry and Shirley Andrews,[14]
P.O. Box 765,
Gold River, BC
V0P 1G0
Tel: (250) 283-7550

## Esperanza Inlet
Josef and Ann Gumpoldsberger, B&B
Box 106, Flynn's Cove,
Zeballos, BC
V0P 2A0
E-mail: flynnscove@direcway.com
Radio tel: (250) 332-5952

### Steamer Point Lodge,
Box 316,
Tahsis, BC
V0P 1X0
Tel: (250) 934-6521

### Tahsis Infobooth (July-Aug. only)
Tel: (250)934-6667

### Zeballos Village Office
Tel: (250)761-4229

# Quick Metric Conversions

## Kyuquot Sound

**BC Parks Strathcona District**
P.O. Box 1479, Highway 19,
Parksville, BC
V9P 2H4
Tel: (250) 954-4600
Fax: (250) 248-8584

**Houpsitas Motel**
Reservations: 1-888-81708716

**Kwa:kwa:tl (Sea otter)**
**Water Taxi Service**
Has a 22 ft covered boat for up to
three kayaks.
E-mail: marilyns@island.net
Tel: (250) 332-5270

**Kyuquot Band Office**
Tel: (250) 332-5259
The Band maintains a list of all cur-
rent water taxis.

**Voyager Water Taxi Service**
Leo Jack has two Coast Guard Auxil-
iary approved and insured boats, fully
covered for bad weather. GPS and radar equipped. Pictures on web site.
www.voyagerwatertaxi.com
Tel: (250) 332-5301 or call them on
VHF Channel 14

**West Coast Expeditions**
www.island.net/~nature
Tel: 1-800-655-3040

**Multiply by**

| | |
|---|---|
| Acres to hectares | 0.4 |
| Hectares to acres | 2.5 |
| | |
| Fathoms to metres | 1.8 |
| Metres to fathoms | 0.6 |
| | |
| Feet to metres | 0.3 |
| Metres to feet | 3.3 |
| | |
| Gallons to litres | 4.6 |
| Litres to gallons | 0.2 |
| | |
| Inches to centimetres | 2.5 |
| Centimetres to inches | 0.4 |
| | |
| Miles to kilometres | 1.6 |
| Kilometres to miles | 0.6 |
| | |
| Nautical miles to kilometres | 1.9 |
| Kilometres to nautical miles | 0.5 |
| | |
| Pounds to kilograms | 0.5 |
| Kilograms to pounds | 2.2 |

Fahrenheit to Celsius
subtract 32, multiply by 5/9

Celsius to fahrenheit
multiply by 9/5, add 32

# Treatment of Hypothermia

Cold water kills. Hypothermia sets in when the body's core temperature drops from the normal 37 °C down to 32 °C resulting in shock followed by cardiac arrest and death at 30 °C.

There have been a few changes to the management of hypothermia in recent years. Consider taking a course in wilderness first aid to be more prepared for what you might encounter in remote areas. The Search and Rescue of B.C. web site, though quite technical, is a good source of up-to-date information. It is www. sarbc.org/andrew1.html. The section on mild hypothermia 34-35 °C is particularly relevant.

## Be Prepared

- Always keep your tarp instantly accessible for when you hit shore

- Always coil tarp guy lines carefully when taking your tarp down—you can't afford the time it takes to untangle them

- Carry a thermos of hot drink

- Carry a stove, even on a day trip

- Carry a sleeping bag or fleece blanket on a day trip

- Get out of the attitude that help is back in town. Set up your trip so that help is right there. Very few situations need evacuation, and you can do more damage in a frantic rush to get out

- An ounce of prevention is worth a ton of cure. Ultimately seamanship and good judgement will prevent

nearly all incidents. Regard being called "chicken" as a compliment

- Be aware of the three stages of hypothermia as the treatment is very different in each

- Wear your PFD at all times

## Symptoms and Treatment

### Mild Symptoms
Pulse is normal – Breathing Normal Appearance: Shivering, slurred speech. Mental state: Conscious

### Treatment
### In the water

- Get as much of the body surface out of the water as possible and that means getting up and over your up-turned kayak or up onto flotsam at once, while you are able to, because you will quickly loose the ability to help yourself (a person loses heat 25 to 30 times faster in water than in air). Find a hat and put it on (we loose a lot of body heat through the head.)

- If someone is rescued and back in the boat, get them working as hard as you can, pumping water out of their boat and then paddling, unless hypothermia is advanced. Steady their boat while they reorganize themselves and stay close beside them until you are absolutely sure that they are no longer hypothermic, Be prepared to tow and have a support kayak each side of them if they become more severely hypothermic before they can get to shore.

- If you can't get out of the water, use the Heat Escape Lessening Position (HELP) Cross your arms tightly across your chest. Draw your knees up close to it. Remain calm and still. Don't swim.

- If others are in the water with you, get into the HUDDLE position: the sides of everyone's chest are close, with arms around mid to lower back and legs intertwined. Put children and elderly people in the centre as they lose heat quicker than others

- The HELP and HUDDLE positions can lengthen survival time in 10 °C water from 2 hours to 4 hours.

**Ashore**
- Use a tarp to get the victim out of the cold, wind and rain

- If one person is hypothermic, look out for others whose body temperature may be going down too. Believe the symptoms not the victim. They'll often tell you they feel fine. This confusion is one of the symptoms.

**Moderate Symptoms**
Pulse slow and weak – Breathing slow and shallow. Appearance: shivering is violent to stopped, clumsy and stumbles. Mental state: Confused, sleepy, irrational.

**Treatment**
- Remove wet clothing and get the person into warm, dry clothing including a warm hat

- Wrap them in a space blanket

- Or alternatively put them in a sleeping bag, pre-warmed if cold (a warm rescuer can get in and prewarm it) meanwhile get well-wrapped warm rocks ready for additional warmth if needed. The old idea of body to body contact is out because the second person could go into hypothermia trying to warm the first.

- Give warm, sweet, non-alcoholic drinks. Never give alcohol. It worsens the situation.

- Protect from the wind and insulate from the ground

- Don't rub the skin. Rubbing extremities brings the warmer core blood to the surface and takes the cold extremity blood back to the core thus intensifying the hypothermia, so rubbing is a no-no.

- Caution the patient not to exercise to re-warm since exercise or activity (other than in the very early stages) also moves cold blood to the core but worse than that the heart becomes very sensitive as hypothermia progresses. Rough handling or exercise can trigger a cardiac arrest.

- For the same reason, handle the person very gently as if they were an egg. This is particularly important when moving or removing wet clothing. Just strip off the outer clothes.

**Severe Symptoms**
Pulse Weak, irregular or absent. Appearance: Shivering has stopped. Mental state: Unconscious.

**Treatment**
- If semiconscious or worse, try to keep the person awake with warm drinks.

- Any rewarming must be as close to the core as possible, warm, sweet non alcohol and non caffeine drinks if conscious. Use heating pads (or fill nalgene water bottles with hot water and wrap in a T-shirt) and put them close to the major arteries to get the core temp. up (between the inner thighs, under the armpits, over the abdomen).

- Monitor breathing and pulse and be prepared to assist either or both if they need it

- If they loose consciousness obtain medical help immediately. Check for heart and breathing regularly **do not** attempt active rewarming unless medical help is delayed but maintain body temperature with insulation (a sleeping bag) and handle them very carefully as the slightest rough handling may cause the heart to stop.

- If signs of circulation are not present give CPR (Cardio Pulmonary Resuscitation) only if it can be maintained without interruption until medical help takes over

- If no medical help is available continue to ventilate (rescue breathing only without the compressions) until the casualty is rewarmed Never assume that a casualty is dead until their body is warm again and there are still no signs of life. Rescue breathing may bring someone back to life who would otherwise have surely died. If it doesn't work, there's nothing else you could have done.

# Historical Chronology

2300 BC Earliest archaeological evidence of human settlement.

1741 Russians Chirikov and Bering explore Alaska and build settlements. Did not venture as far south as Nootka.

1774 Juan Pérez passes Nootka Sound in the *Santiago* but fails to land.

1778 Cook lands at Nootka Sound and claims it for British King George III.

1786 James Charles Strange arrives in *The Experiment*. He leaves his young surgeon, Dr. John Mackay, to write up "...the manners, customs, religion and government of the Nootka."

1787 Captain Charles William Barkley and his wife, Frances, aboard the *Imperial Eagle* purchased furs at Friendly Cove and picked up Dr. John Mackay. She was the first white woman to visit the Pacific Northwest. Barkley Sound is named after them.

1788 John Meares built the *North West America*, the first European ship built on the coast at Friendly Cove. He later claimed to the British Government that he had purchased land from Maquinna.

1789 First Spanish settlement at Nootka under Martínez, who seized the *Iphigenia*, the *North West America* and British *Argonaut* and *Princess Royal*, causing a major international incident in Europe.

1791 Alejandro Malaspina visited Nootka.

1792 Galiano and Valdes continue Malaspina's explorations on behalf of Spain.
Moziño, Spanish botanist-naturalist, wrote *Noticias de Nutka*, a detailed account of life at Nootka April-September 1792.
Vancouver and Quadra attempted unsuccessfully to implement the first Nootka Convention.

1795 Spanish abandoned Nootka

1802-5 John Jewitt's enslavement

1817 French explorer, Roquefeuil, arrived. One of his men discovered traces of the whaler's shrine.

1874-1900 Father A.J. Brabant (1845-1912), a Belgian Roman Catholic priest based at Hesquiat, travelled the coast and visited Friendly Cove.

1885 Government of Canada outlawed the potlatch. This law was not repealed until 1951.

1911 Herbert Smith, an English immigrant, appointed first lightkeeper at Friendly Cove.

1917 Nootka Cannery built

1923 Yuquot designated a National Historic Site by the Canadian Government.

1937 Esperanza Hospital opens.

1938-43 Zeballos gold rush.

1947 Opening of Tahsis sawmill.

1954 Father Brabant's chapel burns down.

1967 Gold River pulp mill opens.

1972 Esperanza Hospital closes.

1999 Gold River Pulp Mill closes.

# Further Reading

Cook, Warren. *Flood Tide of Empire; Spain and the Pacific Northwest* 1543-1819.Yale Univ. Press, 1973 ISBN 0-300-01577-1

Drucker, Philip. *The Northern and Central Nootkan Tribes.* Smithsonian Institution, Bureau of American Ethnology, Bulletin 144, 1951.

Flynn, Bethine. *The Flying Flynns.* N.Y. Seaview, 1979. ISBN 0-87223-538-6

Flynn, Bethine. *Flynn's Cove*, Sidney, Porthole Press, 1986. ISBN 0-919931-10-3

Harbord, Heather. *Nootka Sound and the Surrounding Waters of Maquinna.* Heritage House, 1996. ISBN 1-895811-03-1

Jewitt, John R. *White Slaves of the Nootka; Narrative of the Adventures and Sufferings of John R. Jewitt while a captive on Vancouver Island 1802-1803.* Heritage House, 1987. ISBN 0-919214-51-7

Johnson, Louise. *Not Without Hope; The Story of Dr. H.A. McLean and the Esperanza General Hospital.* Matsqui, Maple Lane. 1992. ISBN 0-921066-02-4

Jones, Laurie. *Nootka Sound Explored; a West Coast History.* Ptarmigan Press, 1991. ISBN 0-919537-24-3

Kenyon, Susan M. *The Kyuquot Way; a Study of a West Coast (Nootkan) Community.* National Museum of Man, Canadian Ethnology Service, Paper No. 61, 1980. ISSN 0316-1854

Lange, Owen S. *The Veil of Chaos. Living with weather along the British Columbia Coast.* Environment Canada. 2003. ISBN 0-660-18984-4

Moziño, Jose Mariano. *Noticias de Nutka. An Account of Nootka Sound in 1792.* Seattle and Vancouver, University of Washington Press and Douglas & McIntyre, 1970. ISBN 0-295-97103-7

# Camping Checklist

**Kayak Equipment**
Kayak
Paddle
Spare paddle
Sponge
Pump
Flares (less than 4 years old)
Paddle Float
Re-entry strap
Heaving line
100 metres fine line for moorage
PFD
Compass
Whistle
6 flares
Paddle float
Pump
Pogies
Spray skirt
Cockpit cover
Wetsuit or Drysuit
Helmet for surf
Thongs
Swellies
Water shoes
Chart case
Charts & tide tables
Carrying straps
Rudder repair kit
Re-entry strap
Deck water
Deck knife

**Cockpit Bag**
Binoculars
Pencil & paper
Sunscreen
Sun glasses
Kleenex
Trail food
Weather radio & spare batteries
VHF & charger
Camera & film
Current book
Wildlife identification books
Star chart
Small waterproof flashlight

**Camping Equipment**
Tent
2 tarps
Thermorest
Underfoam
Sleeping bag
Overbag
Pillow
Small flashlights
Big flashlight
Spare batteries & bulbs
Rope & bear hoist
Crazy Creek Chair
2 large net bags with zips – to reduce trips up and down the beach with small items.

**Clothing etc. in waterproof bags**
Fleece shirt
Lifa underwear (2 sets)
Underwear
Heavy wool socks
Lighter socks
Wind proof pants
Sweat suit
Camp jacket
Toque
Swim suit
Towel
T-shirts
Fleece hat
Hair brush
Alarm clock
Camp shoes
Fleece jacket
Long-sleeved cotton shirt

## Washing gear
Shampoo
First aid kit (incl. Sunscreen)
Hydrogen Peroxide
Insect repellent
Kleenex
Laundry bag
Spare dark glasses
Toilet paper
Trowel
Books
Playing cards

## Clothing – worn or loose
Rain gear
Tilley hat
Paddling jacket
Wind proof pants/shorts

## Kitchen Equipment

(1) Kitchen bag
Stove
Fuel
Matches
Large pot
Cutlery
Can opener
Spatula
Metal whisk
Spices
Tea
Coffee
Hot chocolate
Medication
Mug
Mixing plastic containers
Lemon juice
Biodegradable salt water soap
J cloth & scrubber
Drying-up cloth

Fuel filter funnel
Stove windscreen
First aid kit
Tooth brush & tooth paste
Dental floss
Flashlight
Water purifier
Moist wipes
Pepper & salt
Insect repellent
Toilet paper
Cooking oil
Aluminum foil
Pruner
Purelle hand disinfectant

(2) Heavy cotton bag
Pots & pans
Dishes

(3) Lunch kit
Spare cutlery
Spare can opener
First day's lunch

(4) Water
2 pop bottles on strings
1 collapsible water carrier

(5) Fuel
3 225g cans primus

## Food
Breakfasts & Lunches in 1 bag
Dinners in 1 bag

x breakfasts
y lunches
z suppers
fish fixings
bread makings

# Footnotes

1. Lange, Owen S. *The Veil of Chaos; Living with Weather along the British Columbia Coast.* Environment Canada, 2003. ISBN 0-660-18984-4 p.143

2. http//:lwbc.ca/applying_for_land/commercial_recreation.html

3. All distances are from the turnoff from the Tahsis Road.

4. A slightly longer version of this story first appeared in my 1996 book *Nootka Sound and the Surrounding Waters of Maquinna* on pages 102-3.

5. *Washing of Tears*, NFB film directed by Hugh Brodie.

7. Jewitt, John R. White Slaves of the Nootka; *Narrative of the Adventures and Suffering of John R. Jewitt while a Captive on Vancouver Island.* Heritage House, 1987. ISBN 0-919212-51-7

   *The Adventures and Sufferings of John R. Jewitt, Captive of Chief Maquinna.* Jewitt's narrative annotated and illustrated by Hilary Stewart. Douglas & McIntyre, 1987. ISBN 1-55054-408-X.

8. Unpublished manuscript by Emily Carr entitled *Nootka Had a Hotel*, BCARS Microfilm A1227

10. Flynn, Bethine The Flying Flynns. N.Y. Seaview, 1979. ISBN 0-87223-538-6
    Flynn, Bethine *Flynn's Cove*, Sidney, Porthole Press, 1986. ISBN 0-919931-10-3. Wally died here of a heart attack in 1960.

11. Felch, Alpheus "Explorations of the North-West Coast of the United States; report on the claims of the heirs of Captains Kendrick and Gray." (In Historical Magazine, Boston, Mass., 2nd series, vol.8 (Sept. 1870), pp.155-175

12. This is the tourist arm of the Mowachaht/Muchalaht Band

13. Owner Max Savey is one of the elders of the Mowachaht/Muchalaht Band. As such he has "an in depth knowledge of the area and its history."

14. Larry is a former Chief of the Mowachaht/Muchalaht Band, Shirley was the last teacher on the Friendly Cove Reserve.

# Index

Acous 149, 151, 154, 157-158
Acous Peninsula 154, 157
Ahaminaquus 38-40
Ahmacinnit Island 143, 145
Aktis Island 112, 124, 141, 143-146
Amai Inlet 117-118
Amos Creek 161
Amos Island 120, 134
Argonaut Point 43, 53
Artlish 110, 112-115, 121, 122
Atluk Lake 114
Bajo Point 80, 94-95, 107
Balcom Point 117-118
Battle Bay 112, 149, 154, 157
Beano Creek 54, 58, 80, 96
Belmont Point 78, 80, 87
Benson Point 80, 87-88
Big Bunsby Island 148-149, 151
Big Bunsby Provincial Park 148
Birthday Channel 69-70
Black Rock 97
Bligh Island 35-36, 38, 46, 50
Blowhole Bay 58
Boca del Infierno 35, 55
Bodega Island 58
Boston Point 53, 54-55, 57
Brodick Creek 64, 75
Brooks Peninsula 82-83, 103, 107,
    112, 115, 147-149, 151, 157, 160-162
Bunsby Islands 109-110, 113, 115,
    147-151, 154
Burdwood Bay 50, 52
Burdwood Point 50
Burman River 39-40
Cachalot Inlet 117-118
Caledonia Falls 125-126
Calvin Creek 80, 95
Camel Rock 46
Cameron Rocks 87
Camp Ferrier 80, 92-93, 96
Cape Cook 162
Catala Island 48, 54, 58, 60, 64,
    69-71, 97-99, 101-102, 105, 108, 118
Ceepeecee 60, 65-66, 80
Centre Island 75
Chamiss Bay 123, 127, 153, 155
Charlie's Beach 38, 46

Checkaklis Island 154
Checklakis Island 149, 151
Checleset Bay 150, 152-155,
    157-158, 160
Checleset Ecological Reserve 148
Cheeshish 37, 50
Chutsis Island 119-120
Clanninick Cove 150
Clarke Island 107
Clark Island 130-131
Clear Passage 107, 131
Clerke Peninsula 50, 52
Clerke Point 148, 160-162
Clotchman Island 46
Columbia Cove 157
Colwood Rocks 87
Concepcion Point 50
Coopte Point 53-54
Cougar Creek 37, 38, 42-43, 45-46,
    50, 53
Crawfish Lake 58, 95
Critter Cove 53
Crowther Channel 120, 133-134, 143
Cuttle Islets 154
Descubierta Point 46
Deserted Lake 43
Dixie Cove 117
Double Island 70
Easy Inlet 115, 123, 125-127
Eelstow Passage 115, 123, 125-126
Ehatisaht 60, 67-69
Ehatissaht 60, 69
Eliza Island 104
Ensenada Islet 82
Escalante Beach 52
Esperanza 65, 74, 94
Esperanza Inlet 3, 58-60, 62-63, 65,
    67, 69, 71-72, 74, 75, 79-81, 84-85,
    87, 88, 90, 93, 97, 99, 101-105, 163
Espinosa 71
Espinosa Inlet 60, 62-63, 69-71
Ewing Inlet 52
Expedition Islets 125-126
Fair Harbour 60-62, 68, 110,
    112-122, 125-126
Favourite Entrance 141
Ferrer Point 83, 90, 92-96

Fitz Island 87
Flynn's Cove 76, 172
Flynn Cove 60, 86
Friendly Cove 3, 38, 46-50, 52-55, 57, 61, 66, 68, 86, 94, 96, 99, 103
Garden Point 62, 64, 69, 71-75, 79
Gayward Rock 146
Gay Passage 151, 154
God's Pocket 74
Gold River 3, 8, 15, 35-37, 39-41, 46, 49, 61, 63, 76, 91
Gore Island 41
Grassy Island 107, 130-131
Grassy Knoll 79, 81-87
Graveyard Bay 69-70
Green Head 149, 151, 154
Gross Point 107, 131
Guillod Point 114, 127
Guise Creek 79, 88-89
Hankin Cove 115, 123, 125-126
Hanna Channel 37, 50
Harbour Island 69, 102
Haven Cove 64, 74
Head Bay 45
Hecate Channel 60, 64, 74
High Rocks 100, 105, 108
Hisnet Islands 155
Hisnit Inlet 43-44
Hohoae Island 117, 119-120
Hoiss 3, 38, 53-55
Houston River 41
Inner Basin 88-89
Izard Point 153, 155
Jackobson Point 148-149, 157, 158, 160-161
Jewitt Cove 53-54
Jewitt Lake 56
Johnson Lagoon 158
Jurassic Point 107
Kamils Island 141, 143, 145
Kapoose Creek 105, 107, 115, 129, 131
Kashutl Inlet 125-126
Kate Rocks 136
Kendrick Arm 57-58
Kwois Creek 123, 124
Kyuquot 110, 112, 119-120, 127, 133, 143, 146, 149-150

Kyuquot Sound 12, 110, 113, 115-116, 119, 121-122, 125, 127, 129, 130, 132-133, 135, 140, 143-144, 146, 149, 164
Laurie Creek 88-89
Leiner River 38, 61, 66
Little Espinosa 61-63, 65, 71-72
Little Espinosa Inlet 113, 118
Little Zeballos River 67
Lookout Island 146
Lord Island 88-89
Lord Waterfall 64
Louie Bay 66, 80, 90, 92-93, 96
Lutes Creek 64
Malksope Inlet 149, 150, 152, 155
Malksope Point 150-151
Maquinna Point 96
Markale Passage 119
Markale Peninsula 125
Markale Point 119
Marvinas Bay 53-54
Mary Basin 79, 80, 83, 89, 90
Matchlee 3
Matchlee Bay 39
McBride Bay 60, 74
McCurdy Creek 41
McGrath Point 125
McKay Cove 120, 143
McKay Passage 35, 55
McLean Island 150-151
Mission Group 141, 143-144, 146
Moketas Island 125-126
Monteith Bay 125-127
Moos Islet 136
Mooyah Bay 41
Mount Adair 35, 52
Moutcha Bay 37, 42, 45-46
Moutcha Bay Resort 37
Muchalat Inlet 35, 36, 39-41, 46, 50, 57
Mushroom Point 118, 130
Narvaaz Island 46
Nasparti Inlet 158-159
Nesook Bay 36, 37, 42
Newton Cove 70-72
Nicolaye Channel 133, 143, 146
Nipple Rocks 130

Nootka Island    8, 15, 23, 46, 52-53, 57-58, 60-61, 79-80, 83, 107, 148

Nootka Sound    2, 12, 23, 34-36, 39, 41-48, 50, 52-53, 57, 60, 94, 106-107, 163

Nootka Trail    58, 93, 95

Nuchatlitz    84, 90, 97

Nuchatlitz Inlet    8, 12, 57, 66, 79, 80-81, 83, 91, 94

Nuchatlitz Islands    76, 78, 90, 97

Oclucje    63

Ocluje    60, 62, 70-71, 113

Olebar's Lagoon    150

Otter Island    69-71

Ououkinsh Inlet    153-155

Ous Point    41

Owossitsa Creek    75

Owossitsa Lake    76

Pantoja Islands    35, 52

Peculiar Point    104-105, 108

Peddlar's Cove    149, 156-158, 160

Perpendicular Bluff    45

Pinnace Channel    117

Plumper Harbour    53, 57-58, 96

Port Eliza    60, 69-70, 80, 99, 102, 104-105

Port Langford    78-80, 84-85, 87

Power River    155

Princess Royal Point    45

Queen Cove    60, 66, 69-70, 86, 99, 102, 103, 104

Raccoon Point    133, 135-136

Resolution Cove    35, 50, 52

Resolution Park    62-63, 67, 113

Robin Point    115, 118

Rolling Roadstead    69-70, 99, 102,105

Rolston Island    134

Rosa Island    64, 74, 76, 78, 80-81, 84, 85, 86, 94, 97

Rugged Point    24, 106-107, 110, 112-118, 129-135, 136, 139,

Saavedra islands    46

Saltery Bay    74

Salter Point    53

Santa-Boca Provincial Park    35, 55

Santa Gertrudis Cove    35, 55-56

Santiago Creek    57-58

San Carlos Point    46

Saturnina Point    42

Scarf Island    157

Shelter Sheds    161

Silverado Creek    41

Skirmish Islands    154

Sobry Island    145

Solander Island    148, 160-162

Spanish Pilot Group    46, 52

Spouter Island    35

Spring Island    112, 115, 136-137, 140-144, 146

Steamer Point    65, 74-75

Steamer Point Lodge    65

Strange Island    53-54

Surprise Island    115, 119-120, 127

Tahsis    3, 15, 35-38, 46, 52-53, 57-58, 60-61, 65-67, 76, 91, 122, 163, 168, 172, 176

Tahsish    114-115, 121-124, 126

Tahsish Inlet    114-115, 122-123, 126

Tahsish River    115, 121-124

Tatchu Point    61, 100, 106, 108, 118

Third Beach    79, 93, 95

Thomas Island    150-151

Thornton Islands    135-136, 140-141

Tlupana Inlet    36-37, 43, 45-46, 53

Tongue Point    79-80, 90, 92-93, 95

Tsowwin Narrows    57-58

Tuta Marina    37-38, 50

Twin Islands    97, 101

Union Island    115, 120, 132-133, 136, 141

Upsowis    149, 152-153

Verdia Island    35, 46

Vernaci Island    35

Villaverde Islands    35, 46

Volcanic Islets    130

Walter's Cove    150

Walter's Island    111, 143

West Bay Park    58

Whiteley Island    116, 118

White Cliff Head    133, 135-136

Yaku Bay    123

Yellow Bluff    99, 105-106, 108

Yuquot    35, 40, 47

Zeballos    3, 60-63, 65-68, 83, 86, 113, 163, 176

Zeballos Inlet    60-62

Zuciarte Channel    50, 52

# In Case Of Emergency

In case of an accident, put up one flare and call the Coast Guard on Channel 16. Usually they answer right away. If not, change to channels 6 and 14 can call "any boat close to ...(wherever you are)." Don't let off any further flares until you see a rescue boat looking for you. If the remaining flares are damp, display any set-up featuring a square flag with a ball above or below. A square orange garbage bag weighted down with a black square or circle (rocks) serves the same purpose.

Morse code sound or light signal: A one second sound or flashlight equals a dot and 4-6 seconds equals a dash. S.O.S. consists of three dots, three dashes and three dots.

As the nearest coast guard station is based at Tofino, it may be a while before help appears. Land and make the best of it. Don't expect to be airlifted to a large hospital. Although it's not impossible, you're more likely to be taken to a small centre and then transferred by road.

### Search and Rescue 1-800-663-3456

**Useful Phone Numbers**
Forest Fire Dial '0' and ask for Zenith 5555

Gold River
| | |
|---|---|
| RCMP | (250) 283-2227 |
| Ambulance | 1-800-461-9911 |
| Doctor's Office | (250) 283-2541 |
| Medical Clinic | (250) 283-2626 |
| Fire Department | 1-604-286-8888 |

Tahsis
| | |
|---|---|
| RCMP | (250) 934-6363 |
| Ambulance | 1-800-461-9911 |
| Medical Clinic | (250) 934-6322 |
| Doctor's Office | (250) 934-6912 |
| Fire Emergency | (250) 934-6969 |

Zeballos
| | |
|---|---|
| RCMP (Port McNeill) | (250) 956-4441 |
| Health Unit | (250) 761-4274 |
| Ambulance | 1-800-461-9911 |
| Fire Department | (250) 761-4255 |

Campbell River
| | |
|---|---|
| Hospital | 1-800-287-7111 |